## ALSO BY AL ROKER

*Don't Make Me Stop This Car!*

# AL ROKER'S
# BIG BAD BOOK
# OF BARBECUE

### 100 Easy Recipes for Backyard
### BARBECUE *and* GRILLING

## AL ROKER

### PHOTOGRAPHS BY MARK THOMAS

**Scribner**

*NEW YORK LONDON TORONTO SYDNEY SINGAPORE*

SCRIBNER

A Division of Simon & Schuster, Inc.
1230 Avenue of the Americas
New York, NY 10020

First Scribner trade paperback edition June 2008

SCRIBNER and design are registered trademarks of The Gale Group, Inc.,
used under license by Simon & Schuster, Inc., the publisher of this work.

For information about special discounts for bulk purchases,
please contact Simon & Schuster Special Sales:
1-800-456-6798 or business@simonandschuster.com

Designed by Barbara Bachman

Illustrations by Mary Fris

Text set in Trade Gothic and Grotesque

Manufactured in the United States of America

1  3  5  7  9  10  8  6  4  2

Library of Congress Control Number: 2002066789

ISBN-13: 978-1-4165-9538-0

ISBN-10: 1-4165-9538-4

This book is dedicated to the memory of my father,

## Albert L. Roker, Sr.

Without his insatiable curiosity about cooking, I don't think

I would have the love of preparing food that has driven me

to experiment, to have fun, and to enjoy what I do,

whether it's in the kitchen, the backyard, or on television.

# Acknowledgments

I WOULD LIKE TO THANK THE FOLLOWING FOLKS:

Once again, a big thank-you to my nifty Simon & Schuster editor, Trish Todd, for helping move this thing along. I'd also like to thank Rica Allannic and Beth Wareham at Scribner for their invaluable help in shepherding the project.

Tekella Miller and Cressida Suttles at Al Roker Productions helped keep me on track. And a *huge* thank-you to my wife, Deborah Roberts, for putting up with my obsession with grilling and barbecue. Honest, sweetie, the smoky smell will come out of the drapes!

# Contents

# Introduction

**M**y late father stands out in my earliest memories of grilling. This was in the early 1960s. There were no fancy grillers, smokers, and barbecue pits. Nope. Al Roker, Sr., had one of those inverted flying-saucer grills with the three-leg setup. Probably cost $12.99. The charcoal briquettes cost more than the grill did.

He would drag that grill out into our backyard in St. Albans, Queens, and we knew what that meant. FIRE! When it came to the manly art of fire building, Dad's theory was that if a little charcoal lighter fluid was good, then a lot was great.

Al Senior would pick up the rectangular metal can, pop the top off, and squeeze. And squeeze. You could leave the backyard, go to the bathroom, finish up, head back downstairs, stop in the kitchen, get a soda, and return to the backyard, and he'd still be squeezing.

When the briquettes were soaked to his satisfaction, Dad would back up about twenty feet, toss a lighted match in the general direction of the grill, and WHOOOOOOMPPP!!!! A fireball visible to the *Apollo* astronauts would rise from our back-yard. "Now, that's a fire!" Dad would exclaim, grinning from ear to ear.

All this to incinerate a few pre-cooked hot dogs and hand-patted burgers. It wasn't that Dad was a bad cook. On the contrary, he was an excellent cook. You could make the argument that my father was a better cook than my mom.

The problem was that my father was a social cook. He would start cooking and before you could say "The burgers are on fire!" he would be chatting with neighbors over the fence about the New York Mets, Mayor Lindsay, or the state of the New York City Transit system, where he worked as a bus driver. As far as he was concerned, the best part about a cookout was meeting and greeting. It was hanging out with your friends and family in a relaxed atmosphere. In our house, barbecue was a euphemism for "Get me another beer."

That's what grilling and barbecue is all about. It is the most social of the cooking arts. You are in the great outdoors with family and friends, cooking and talking. You connect with people in ways you don't in a more formal setting like a dining room or cocktail party. Children are usually running around, chasing each other or family pets. Old friends are shooting the bull and new friends are being made.

We enjoyed the smell of the food cooking and the closeness we shared with our parents on our back porch. We would play cards or Monopoly, waiting for the burgers to cook. I think that's why I am so drawn to grilling and barbecuing today. It's what my father did. I think that's why the person in front of the grill is usually a guy. It's what our dads did. That's not to say women don't grill. They do. In fact, according to the Barbecue Industry Association, 27% of all grillers are women. While that doesn't sound like many, the number is up considerably from just ten years ago.

I remember the first time I was allowed to cook the food on the grill. I was twelve years old. Dad gave me the tongs and let me pile up the charcoal briquettes and pour on the lighter fluid. I got to set off the traditional fireball and cook the hot dogs. It was as much a passage into manhood as driving the family station wagon or passing out in a bar in midtown Manhattan and waking up wearing women's clothing somewhere near Exit 8 on the Jersey Turnpike . . . but that's another story.

When I was in college, my roommates and I had a tiny hibachi that we would take out by the lake. Normal food tastes so much better when it's cooked over an open fire. We actually made grilled cheese sandwiches on that hibachi. You feel connected to nature when you're grilling outside. Not as connected as when you realize the place you've chosen to "take care of business" is in the middle of a patch of poison sumac, but connected nonetheless.

So why am I, Al Roker, qualified to write a book on grilling and barbecue? Actually, I'm no more qualified than you are, if you love the smell of wood smoke, or the hissing of food cooking over a fire, or the pop of hot fat hitting the flames.

They say you should always write about what you know. I always wonder who "they" are. Deborah, my wife, sometimes remarks, "They say it's going to be chilly tomorrow." I look at her and reply, "Oh, really? Hello . . . I knew that. Why? I'm 'they.' I'm a weatherman!" But I digress. I have always had this love of grilling and barbecuing smoldering in my veins.

It burst into a full-blown forest fire three years ago when I did a Food Network special on the Memphis in May Barbecue Championship held every year on the banks of the Mississippi River in Memphis, Tennessee. It's a mecca for those who worship at the altar of barbecue. Professionals and amateurs trade secrets about rubs, sauces, and techniques while vying for different prizes in the world of barbecue: Best Ribs, Best

Whole Hog, Best Sauce, Best Non-Pork Barbecue. When I got to Memphis, I knew a little about barbecue; I knew what tasted good. Then, for three days, I talked with barbecue legends like John Willingham and the Neely brothers, folks who own working barbecue joints in and around Memphis. I hung out with teams competing for both professional and amateur titles. When I left Memphis, I came away with a fire in my belly, and it wasn't the baked beans. It was a newfound love of this truly American cuisine.

I had a new appreciation for a style of cooking that has been underappreciated for years. How many times did I eat what I thought were barbecued ribs when, in fact, I had been devouring ribs that had been boiled, finished off underneath a broiler, and slathered with a candy-sweet sauce that had some Liquid Smoke in it. Do you know how to tell if the ribs you're eating are really, truly slow cooked, infused with the perfume of wood smoke? Cut the ribs apart and look at the meat. If you see a pink ring around the inside of the meat, that means it has been slow cooked. The smoke creates that ring, and the smoke adds the flavor.

Since my Memphis epiphany, I've used a lot of barbecue cookbooks. My favorites are covered with grease, sauce, and stuff I can't even identify because I use them so much and have them next to me as I cook. Cookbooks that encourage me to go off on my own and push me to try new things are the ones I love best. I don't want something that makes me feel like an idiot. I don't want to look at a recipe and say, "Well, if I had a couple of days, I might be able to pull this off." Or, "If I was able to assemble a kick-butt cooking team, I'd have a shot at creating this."

I've tried to come up with a book that you'll really *use.* Let's face it. We're talking about grilling and barbecuing here. This is not rocket science. Although if you try some of those commercial sauces out there, you'll find they taste like rocket fuel. This book is about starting your own traditions. Making your own way in the world of barbecue and grilling.

I'm no chef, but I love cooking on the grill, and I've learned a thing or two along the way. So how did I come up with these recipes? I found somebody who loves barbecue and grilling as much as I do and got her to take some of my ideas and what I've learned and put it down so that other people could make the same things I serve my family and friends.

Marialisa Calta is a wonderful cook, recipe writer, and food columnist. She writes a weekly column that is syndicated in more than a hundred papers across the country and has written a few cookbooks, including the *River Run Cookbook.* She also knows how to create recipes. We spent a lot of time together, talking about what I like to eat and how I cook and what I cook. I would describe my mother's peas and rice, or Deborah's potato salad. She would divine the ingredients that might be missing from my recipe and fill in the blanks. We talked about dishes I make and how I make them. In some sort of scientific, secret way, she conjured up the recipes and the ingredients and has written a road map for what I call "foolin' around" in the kitchen or at the grill. And now she knows how to create recipes that feed six. I kept asking her, "Marialisa, you mean feeds six normal people, or six people like my friends and family? In that case, double everything!"

I could not have produced this book without her and want to acknowledge her contribution to it.

Now I have deeper respect and appreciation for what goes into creating a cookbook: the writing, the editing, the photography that looks good enough to eat.

I guess I've always wanted to write a cookbook, to be able to help people make meals that they would be proud to serve to family and friends. After all, that's what cooking is all about. It means you care. We equate home cooking with love. I look at barbecue and grilling as a representation of love in edible form.

I want to help you give the people you care about a whole lotta love.

# AL ROKER'S
## BIG BAD BOOK
## OF BARBECUE

# Al's Guide to Grilling

## Gas vs. Charcoal

All right. Let's get down to it. We can argue about whether you like your ribs "wet" or "dry." We can debate the merits of pork as opposed to beef barbecue. I may even cave in and put my veggies in one of those cute little baskets instead of just slapping them right on the grill.

Nothing, and I mean nothing, gets people going like the argument of gas vs. charcoal. I will state, right up front, I am not crazy about gas grills—and not for the reasons you think. Granted, I do fall into the category of those who believe that charcoal-grilled food just plain tastes better. I know that you can put the wood chip smoker boxy things in the gas grill and you'll never know the difference, right? Right!

No, that's not my beef, pardon the pun, with gas grills. Everyone who waxes poetic about their gas grill extols the speed with which they can cook a meal. No muss, no fuss, just the flick of a switch and you're grilling.

*That's* my problem with gas grills. My feeling is that we rush so many things today;

we don't take time to enjoy the simple pleasures of life. Ritual is as much a part of bar-becuing and grilling as eating is. As I am writing this, I am sitting in my backyard in the country, looking at my three Weber kettles. There's not a gas grill to be seen. The clos-est these grills get to gas is when I've tasted the baked beans before I start cooking on the kettles.

In the interest of full disclosure, I admit that I do own a gas grill. It's behind my brownstone in Manhattan. I bought a gas grill for the city because I figure the quicker I'm on and off the grill, the less our smoke and flames will affect our neighbors. But every time I look at our gas grill, I miss my kettles.

But arguing against gas grills is swimming against the tide. In 2001, 60% of all new grills sold were gas, as opposed to 40% charcoal. People want the ease and lack of mess that gas grills represent. But some things can't be rushed, nor should they be.

## Charcoal Briquettes vs. Hardwood Lump Charcoal

I'm a purist about one other thing: I don't use charcoal briquettes. They're made of hard-wood, wood scraps, and petroleum binders. In fact, did you know that automobile man-ufacturer Henry Ford was responsible for the invention of the charcoal briquette as we know it today?

Ford's "Woody" Station Wagon and other wood products for Ford automobiles were made in a plant in Kingsford, Michigan. To make use of all the waste wood the plant generated, Ford built a chemical plant in 1924. For every ton of wood used at the plant, 610 pounds of charcoal briquettes were reclaimed. Hence, Kingsford Charcoal Briquettes became the first nationally known brand of charcoal briquette.

Although briquettes are a fine product, I try to avoid them because you have to wait for the briquettes to "ash over" before you use them. And if you're cooking for a while and want to add more briquettes to keep the heat up, then you have to wait for the new briquettes to ash over.

I use hardwood lump charcoal, which is what you get when you burn hardwood like oak or maple in the absence of oxygen. What's left is charcoal. It burns cleaner and hotter than briquettes. When you get your fire going with hardwood lump charcoal, it is ready to go immediately. And when you have to add charcoal to the fire, there's no need to wait for it to ash over.

It used to be hard to find hardwood lump charcoal. You'd have to go to a specialty store or special order it from your hardware store. Now, almost every chain grocery and hardware store carries hardwood lump charcoal.

## Wood Chips

But hardwood lump charcoal itself doesn't give you that great smoky flavor that we all associate with barbecue and grilling. You can buy the more flavorful mesquite, hickory, or maple at your local gourmet grocery or hardware store, or you can look in specialty stores for more exotic woods like fig tree wood, wine barrel wood, and grapevine cuttings. Just soak the chips in water for about half an hour (chunks for an hour), drain them, then throw them on the coals. (If you're using a gas grill, put them in the grill's smoker box.)

One of my favorite places to get different flavored woods is called Peoples Woods (see Sources, page 189). Located in Rhode Island, they started by selling coal. But to try to make a little cash during the warm weather months, they went into selling all kinds of wood products for grilling and barbecue. They sell over a dozen different kinds of wood chunks and chips.

## Utensils

You can walk up and down the aisles of your local gourmet store and find tons of stuff made for the barbecue enthusiast. "Professional" barbecue utensils in cases that look like those Halliburton brushed aluminum attachés make me laugh. As if they only sell them to "professionals," but they'll slip you one for the right price . . .

C'mon. Here's what you need to barbecue. You might want to take notes, because this is really complicated . . . Not!

A GRILL. Gas, charcoal, whatever. As I said, I'm partial to charcoal, but whatever floats your boat is okay with me. I still maintain that if you're grilling with gas, you may as well slap your meat under the broiler in the kitchen. But that's just me.

Maybe you've seen those catalogs selling the professional grills. These rigs cost more than my first car and have more chrome and stainless steel on them to boot. A simple grill, kettle or otherwise, gets the job done. I've had barbecue from a converted fifty-five-gallon drum that was so good "you'd slap your momma." I've been told that slapping your momma is a real compliment to a cook . . . Unless the cook is your momma, then if your momma's like my momma, you'd better run.

The point is, it's not about fancy. You can do some very good backyard cooking on a rig that won't require a mortgage.

**THINGS TO MOVE YOUR MEAT AROUND THE GRILL.** Yeah, I've seen the fancy-handled tongs and forks, with the matching corncob holders and salt and pepper shakers. When anybody pulls one of those out at a backyard cooking session, I always think: "Oooo, too much. This is probably someone who alphabetizes his CD collection." Although, as Deborah would point out, I have my DVDs cross-referenced by director, genre, and title, so I have no right to talk.

All you really need are two things: a good pair of long tongs to grab your steak, chicken, or fish and move it around on the grill, and a long spatula to flip burgers, veggies, and chicken parts. I find those are the two utensils I use the most when I'm grilling. Make sure the handles are well insulated, don't conduct heat, and are long enough for you to stand at a comfortable distance from the grill. Keep them clean and they will pay for themselves many times over. Plus you can use 'em in the kitchen when you're not grilling so that you can think about grilling even when you're not.

**MITTS.** You could also use a good pair of insulated mitts to make sure you don't burn your hands or forearms when you're close to the grill manipulating whatever it is you're cooking. There's nothing worse than realizing that tantalizing smell is . . . you!

**A MOP.** I'm not talking about what you'll use to clean up with after everyone goes home. I'm talking about the tool you use to splash on your basting sauce, also called "mop." Sound like a bad Abbott and Costello routine? Not really. "Mopping" sauce got its name when barbecue pit masters used an actual mop to slap the sauce onto a roasting pig. Today, for those of us using a smaller cut of meat, like a pork butt or ribs, we like to use a smaller mop for the sauce. You can buy a small glass mop, normally used to wash fine glasses. I find it makes a great mop to slap my mop onto my meat. Who's on first? I don't know. Third base!

A THERMOMETER. I'm a big fan of these new digital thermometers. I have one that costs less than thirty dollars. It's got a long cord attached to a probe that you can put inside the grill if the top is down and you want to regulate the temperature as you would with an oven. Or you can place the probe into your beef, pork, or chicken to see if it's reached the proper internal temperature. The readings appear on a little console attached to the other end of the cord. It has a nifty magnetic base that keeps it anchored to the grill's base or a table.

## Meat

Let me say one thing about selecting your meat. Try to buy the best quality that you can afford. You don't have to buy filet mignon when buying steak: (a) it's not that good a grilling meat and (b) it's just too darn expensive.

Make friends with your butcher. Here in Manhattan, there are some very high-end butchers that will only see you by appointment and with two references and a bank statement. But guess what? If you go to your local chain-store butcher, ring the bell, and wait for someone to slide the window open, you'll find a friend. Why? Because chances are, he'll be excited about the idea that someone else is into red meat. If you ask him to cut something special, it gives the butcher a chance to be appreciated and, dare I say it . . . loved.

A few of my favorite local butchers in New York City are Citarella on the East and West Side, Agata and Valentina on the Upper East Side, and Fairway in Harlem. When

I'm grilling at our house in Upstate New York, the butcher at the Chatham Market supplies my meat, as does Mazzeo's Meat Market at Guido's in Pittsfield, Massachusetts.

## Starting the Fire

I love the ritual of getting the fire going on a charcoal grill. Lighter fluid? We don't need no stinkin' lighter fluid. About fifteen years ago, I saw a guy use a homemade chimney starter. It was a coffee can with a handle stuck in it, and some hanger wire stuck through about three-quarters of the way down. I watched as he put some newspaper in the bottom, then poured his charcoal in the top. He placed the whole thing on top of the charcoal grate of his grill and lit a match under the bottom. Within fifteen minutes, his coals were ready and he started cooking.

Today, you can buy ready-made charcoal chimneys, eliminating the need for lighter fluid and that petroleum taste it gives your burgers. Granted, you give up the possibility of the famed Al Roker, Sr., fireball, but your insurance premiums will stay low.

## Heat: High vs. Low and Direct vs. Indirect

So you've dumped your hot coals into the grill (or you've preheated your gas grill to "singe") and you're all fired up and ready to grill, right? Maybe. Seems like common sense, but I've gotta say it: read the recipe. If you're cooking hot dogs, odds are your recipe calls for grilling over "direct, high heat" and you're good to go. But if you're making, let's say, a rack of ribs, you'll need "indirect, low heat" so that the ribs can cook for a long time instead of charring right off the bat.

So there are two things going on here: the position of the heat source and how blistering the blast is. "Direct" grilling is done right over the coals or fire. Arrange an even layer of coals in your grill or preheat your gas grill uniformly. For "indirect" grilling, divide your coals in half (or light your gas grill on the sides or, on a two-burner grill, on one side), leaving an empty space in the center of the grill. If using coals, put a disposable aluminum drip pan in the center before adding the cooking grate. Put the food over the empty spot so that it cooks slowly and evenly without burning.

For the second part of the equation—that is, how hot your fire is—I'm sure you've read about the ways to check the heat level. Hold your hand a few inches over the grill surface. If you can keep it there for a minute or two, odds are your fire is out. Can you keep it there for somewhere between ten and fifteen seconds? It's probably a low heat. More like five to ten seconds? Then you've got a medium-heat fire. Only a few seconds, and you're looking at the high heat . . . especially if you're Roger Clemens. If in a second or less your hand catches fire, then that's really high heat or you're G. Gordon Liddy.

You can also adjust the heat on some grills by moving the grilling rack down so that the food is closer to the fire and gets a real surge of heat, or up so that the food is further from the fire and gets more gentle warmth. For a hotter fire on a charcoal grill, pile up the coals in a thick, double layer. For more moderate heat, spread a single layer of coals on the grate.

I think you can tell pretty easily how hot your fire is. If you can smelt iron ore, I think your fire might be a little too hot. Even so, all fires start to lose their oomph after a while. It's a good idea to check on your coals about an hour into your grilling time. If your fire is more gray ash than glowing embers, add more fuel. Pull out your chimney starter, if you use one, to heat additional coals. Otherwise, just add the new coals to the grill on top of the old ones. They will take a little while to heat up and may smoke a bit in the process, but they'll do the trick.

If your grill has a cover, use it (remember to open the vents on a charcoal grill). All the recipes in my book that call for cooking longer than five minutes were tested with the top on. If going topless, you may need to adjust the cooking times. (A cover is essential, though, for slow-cooked recipes such as brisket and pulled pork.)

Finally, get to know your grill! All grills are different, and you should read the directions that come with yours (if you can find them). But trust me, you'll get the hang of this. And if your steak takes a little longer to cook than you'd planned, pour yourself another glass of something, kick back, and enjoy the afternoon.

## Grill Temperatures

*If you're a stickler for details and want to bust out your probe thermometer to measure the intensity of your fire, here's a rough guide of what you're looking for:*

| | |
|---|---|
| High Heat | 450–500 degrees F and up |
| Medium Heat | about 350 degrees F |
| Low Heat | 250–300 degrees F |

# Al Roker's Five Rules of Grilling and Barbecue

1. **NEVER TOUCH ANOTHER MAN'S GRILL.** I will be the first to admit that when it comes to cooking, I'm a bit of a control freak. I love folks hanging out in the kitchen while I cook, but I don't want any help. The same holds true at the backyard grill. Don't ask to help me cook. I would never think of touching your grill. I know that every inch of soot-and-grease-encrusted metal has been lovingly and patiently created by you. It's one of the manly arts. Ever heard of the old saying "Too many cooks spoil the broth?" Here's another one: "Touch my grill or any of my utensils, they'll be calling you 'Stumpy'!"

2. **DO NOT USE A FORK TO MOVE YOUR MEAT AROUND THE GRILL.** Use tongs. If you pierce the meat with a fork, all those wonderful juices will run out onto the coals, cause some wonderful flare-ups, and leave you with grilled shoe leather. While your friends "Oooooo" and "Aaahhh" at the flames, you're ruining your meat and run the risk of setting your facial hair on fire. Wanna hear people go "Oooooo" and "Aaaahhhhh"?

3. **DON'T KEEP MOVING YOUR MEAT AROUND THE GRILL.** Once you slap it on the grill, just leave it, unless it either: (a) starts to burn and you have to move it to a cooler spot or (b) there's inclement weather and you are threatened by floods, locusts, lightning, or all of the above. It may be very satisfying to flip your burger and push it down on the grill. Know what that does? Causes flare-ups and dries out the meat. See Rule 2.

4. **DO NOT WEAR AN APRON THAT SAYS "KISS THE COOK."** If you want to invite ridicule, scorn, and derision, then by all means, wear something like the aforementioned apron or like attire. By the same token, I always love those pictures of barbecues in the glossy food magazines with people wearing designer sweaters tied around their necks and khaki slacks or skirts. Who are these people? What kind of barbecue are they at? They probably eat ribs with a knife and fork! Me, I love grilling in an old T-shirt and shorts. In fact, I usually wear those sport shorts that are good on land and water. If things get a little hot, I take a break from grilling and jump in the pool. But not for long, lest somebody think the grill needs tending. See Rule 1.

5. **DON'T TAKE IT TOO SERIOUSLY.** Enjoy yourself. That's the deal with grilling and barbecue. Friends and family. Laughter and good times. It's not like being at those trendy downtown bars, where everyone is dressed in black and they all look like they need a cookie. Backyard cooking is folks who look like you and me, people we know, but more important, people we want to hang out with.

# Start Your Engines

# Guacamole

Don't try to make this more than 2 hours in advance; it will turn a very unappealing shade of brown. Of course, if the color scheme of your party is earth tones, then by all means make this dish a day early.

---

3 ripe avocados
3 tablespoons freshly squeezed lime
   juice (from 1 to 2 limes)
1/2 large tomato, stemmed
1/2 large onion, peeled and finely
   chopped
2 cloves garlic, peeled and minced

1/2 jalapeño pepper, stemmed, seeded,
   and finely chopped
1/2 cup chopped cilantro leaves
1 teaspoon coarse salt, such as
   kosher salt
Freshly cracked pepper

---

1 • Using a sharp knife, cut the avocados in half. Remove the pits. Scoop the flesh into a medium bowl and roughly crush with a potato masher or fork. Stir in the lime juice.

2 • Chop the tomato as finely as possible. Scrape the tomato flesh and juice into the bowl with the avocados.

3 • Add the onion, garlic, jalapeño pepper, cilantro, salt, and pepper and stir to mix.

4 • Press a sheet of plastic wrap on the surface of the guacamole. Let sit for about 30 minutes at room temperature and then adjust the seasonings; you may want to add more jalapeño pepper, lime juice, salt, or pepper.

5 • Serve at room temperature with tortilla chips for dipping.

*Makes about 3 cups, or 8 servings*

# Salsa, Two Ways

There are a lot of good store-bought salsas, but nothing beats the bright flavors of homemade. I also think folks are mighty impressed that you took the time to make salsa from scratch. There are other ways to cut corners for dips using store-bought items, and we'll talk about those later.

This basic salsa can be flavored either of two ways: for cilantro lovers, add the fresh herb; for others, add the cumin. (You could also split the batch and serve half one way and half the other; just remember to halve the amounts of cilantro and cumin.)

You can make this in a food processor if you like fairly smooth salsa, or you can chop everything by hand for a rougher texture. I prefer the rougher texture. Get some of those folks who like helping you in the kitchen or by the grill and enlist them to chop up the ingredients. It will keep them busy and out of your hair for a while.

6 very ripe, medium tomatoes
   (2 pounds), stemmed
1 medium green bell pepper, stemmed
   and seeded
1/2 medium red onion, peeled
1 jalapeño pepper, stemmed and seeded
3 cloves garlic, peeled
2 teaspoons extra-virgin olive oil

2 teaspoons cider vinegar
2 teaspoons freshly squeezed lime juice
   (from 1 lime)
3/4 teaspoon salt
1/4 teaspoon cayenne pepper
1/2 cup chopped cilantro leaves, or
   2 teaspoons ground cumin

1 • *If working by hand,* chop the tomatoes as finely as possible. Scrape the tomato flesh and juice into a bowl. Chop the green pepper, onion, jalapeño pepper, and garlic as finely as possible. Scrape into the bowl with the tomatoes.

*If using a food processor,* chop the tomatoes into chunks and then put them in the work bowl. Puree until fairly smooth; the tomatoes will be soupy but still a bit lumpy. Let the tomatoes drain in a colander or strainer for a couple of minutes to reduce the liquid. Transfer the tomatoes to a bowl. Cut the green pepper, onion, and jalapeño pepper into chunks. Put them in the bowl of the food processor with the garlic and pulse until finely chopped. Scrape into the bowl with the tomatoes.

2 • Whichever method you used, now add the oil, vinegar, lime juice, salt, and cayenne to the tomatoes. Stir in the cilantro or the cumin.

3 • Let the salsa sit at room temperature for at least 1 hour for the flavors to blend. Taste and adjust the seasonings; you may want to add more vinegar, salt, or cayenne, as well as more cilantro or cumin.

4 • This is best served the day you make it, but you can keep the salsa for up to 2 days in a covered container in the refrigerator. Serve with tortilla chips.

*Makes about 4 cups, or 12 servings*

# Black Bean Dip

This dip is low in fat. Like you really care. Here's the deal: I've placed several "healthy" recipes in here so that my wife will not give me a hard time. Yes, we have to watch our fat intake and watch the cholesterol and yada yada yada. So, if someone who loves you starts complaining about another barbecue book, tell 'em Al's wife, who is a size 4, approved of this recipe—if not the whole book.

2 (15½-ounce) cans black beans, drained, rinsed, and drained again
1 cup chopped cilantro leaves
2 tablespoons finely grated orange zest (from 2 oranges)
⅓ cup freshly squeezed orange juice (from 1 orange)

¼ cup canola oil, or other vegetable oil
1 teaspoon salt
Several dashes Louisiana-style hot sauce

1 • Put all of the ingredients in the work bowl of a food processor or in a blender (you may have to do this in 2 batches if using a blender), and puree until smooth. Transfer to a bowl and let sit for at least 30 minutes for the flavors to blend. Taste and add more salt or hot sauce, if desired.

2 • This is best served the day you make it, but you can keep the dip for up to 2 days in a covered container in the refrigerator. Serve at room temperature with wedges of pita bread.

*Makes about 3 cups, or 8 servings*

# Chile-Olive Dip

This is especially good as an accompaniment to London Broil (page 48) made with Southwestern Marinade (page 167).

1 cup sour cream
1 (4-ounce) can peeled, mild green
    chiles (not jalapeño peppers, unless
    you want the dip to be very hot)
1 (3³/4-ounce) jar pimento-stuffed green
    olives, drained (about
    1/2 cup)

¹/3 cup mayonnaise
1 clove garlic, peeled and minced
1 teaspoon chili powder
¹/2 teaspoon salt
¹/4 teaspoon ground cumin
Freshly ground pepper

1 • Place all of the ingredients in the work bowl of a food processor or in a blender, and puree until smooth. Cover and refrigerate for at least 1 hour and up to 24 hours.

2 • Serve with chips—corn chips are best—cherry tomatoes, and sliced raw vegetables.

*Makes about 2 cups, or 6 servings*

# Clam-Bacon Dip

This is great if you're at the beach and have extra steamers.

---

3 slices thick-cut bacon, or 4 slices
    regular bacon
½ medium onion, peeled and cut into
    chunks
½ red bell pepper, stemmed, seeded,
    and cut into chunks
1 cup fresh minced clams (available in
    the fish department of most super-
    markets), or canned clams, drained

8 ounces cream cheese, at room
    temperature
1 cup sour cream
2 tablespoons chopped parsley
1 tablespoon freshly squeezed lemon
    juice (from 1 lemon)
A few drops Worcestershire sauce

---

1 • Warm a skillet over medium-high heat. Add the bacon and cook, turning as needed until crisp, 12 to 15 minutes. Remove the bacon from the skillet and drain on paper towels. When it's cool, chop or crumble finely and set aside.

2 • *If using a food processor,* put the onion and bell pepper in the work bowl and pulse until finely chopped. Add the clams, cream cheese, sour cream, parsley, lemon juice, and Worcestershire sauce, and process until the mixture is like a dip in consistency. It should still be chunky.

   *If working by hand,* chop the onion and bell pepper finely. Set aside. In a bowl, beat the cream cheese with a wooden spoon until very soft. Add the onion and bell pepper, clams, sour cream, parsley, lemon juice, and Worcestershire sauce, and stir vigorously.

3 • Transfer the dip to a serving bowl, and stir in the chopped bacon. Cover and refrigerate for at least 30 minutes, and up to 24 hours, for the flavors to blend.

4 • Serve well chilled with potato chips or sliced raw vegetables.

*Makes about 3 cups, or 10 servings*

# Spinach-Yogurt Dip

Here's another recipe that you can easily adapt to a low-fat or nonfat version. Nonfat yogurt and sour cream work just as well. Not as much fun, but at least they give you an alternative.

| | |
|---|---|
| 1 (10-ounce) package frozen chopped spinach, thawed | 1 cup plain yogurt |
| 1/2 small onion, peeled and halved | 1 cup sour cream |
| 2 cloves garlic, peeled | 1/2 teaspoon salt |
| | Freshly ground pepper |

1 • Put the spinach in a colander and, using your hands or the back of a spoon, squeeze out as much liquid as possible. Set the spinach aside.

2 • *If using a food processor,* put the onion and garlic in the bowl and pulse until finely chopped. Add the yogurt, sour cream, salt, pepper, and the spinach, and puree until smooth.
*If using a blender,* chop the onion and garlic roughly by hand, then put in the blender along with the remaining ingredients. Process until smooth.

3 • Cover and refrigerate for at least 1 hour or up to 24 hours before serving. Serve with sliced raw vegetables and wedges of pita bread.

*Makes about 3 cups, or 8 servings*

## Quick Starters

*Sometimes you've spent so much time on the main meal that you don't want to work too hard on the munchies. These dips are quickly assembled with store-bought ingredients.*

**Store-Bought Salsa and Sour Cream Dip:** Mix 2 parts salsa with 1 part sour cream (or to taste). Serve with tortilla chips.

**Cream Cheese and Jalapeño Pepper Jelly Spread:** Spoon 1 cup of jalapeño pepper jelly (available in supermarkets) on top of a softened, 8-ounce brick of cream cheese. Serve with crackers.

**Homemade Onion Dip:** Finely chop an onion and sauté it in a bit of oil until translucent, about 10 minutes. Add 2 tablespoons instant beef bouillon powder. Cool, then stir into 2 cups sour cream, along with several dashes Worcestershire sauce. Serve with potato chips and sliced raw vegetables.

**Tapenade-Yogurt Dip:** Mix equal portions store-bought tapenade (olive spread) with plain yogurt. Serve with spears of fresh vegetables.

**Anchovy Dip:** Drain and finely chop a 2.2-ounce tin of anchovies; combine with $1/2$ cup sour cream and $1/2$ cup mayonnaise. Add some chopped parsley and 1 to 2 cloves minced garlic. Serve with sliced raw vegetables or pita bread, but *not* with salty chips.

# BBQ Popcorn

Think of this subtly addictive mix as barbecued caramel corn. Your guests won't even miss the prize.

---

*½ cup popcorn kernels, or 1 (3-ounce) packet "94% fat-free" microwave popcorn*
*¼ cup canola oil, or other vegetable oil (for stovetop popping only)*

*6 tablespoons (¾ stick) unsalted butter*
*2½ tablespoons BBQ Rub (page 174)*
*1 tablespoon Louisiana-style hot sauce*
*2 cups honey-roasted peanuts*

---

1 • *If using an air-popper,* you will not need the oil; pop according to the manufacturer's instructions. *If popping on the stovetop,* heat the oil and 2 or 3 kernels of corn in a heavy, covered saucepan set over medium-high heat. When the kernels pop, add the rest of the corn. Cover the pan and, using a potholder, hold the lid down and shake the pan as the kernels pop. *If using microwave popcorn,* follow the package directions.

2 • Melt the butter in a saucepan set over low heat. Add the rub and hot sauce, and cook, stirring, for about 5 minutes, until the rub is dissolved and well blended into the butter.

3 • Put the warm popcorn in a large bowl. Pour the seasoned butter on top and toss to coat. Add the peanuts, but don't stir them in; as people grab handfuls of popcorn the nuts will sink to the bottom (just like the peanuts in a box of caramel corn).

*Makes about 10 cups, or 8 servings*

# Spicy Gazpacho

I love gazpacho. It is the perfect starter on a warm summer afternoon. Here's a dish that's okay to make ahead of time. In fact, make it a day ahead. It's one less thing you've gotta worry about on the day of the barbecue, *and* the flavors get a chance to blend.

1 ear fresh corn, husked, or 1 cup
   frozen corn
1/2 medium red onion, peeled and cut
   into chunks
2 cloves garlic, peeled
1/2 medium green bell pepper,
   stemmed, seeded, and cut into
   chunks
1/2 medium red bell pepper, stemmed,
   seeded, and cut into chunks
1 to 2 jalapeño peppers, according to
   taste, stemmed and seeded
16 ripe plum tomatoes (about 2 1/2
   pounds), stemmed and cut into
   chunks

3 tablespoons cider vinegar
2 tablespoons chopped cilantro leaves,
   plus extra whole leaves for garnish
2 tablespoons sugar
1 tablespoon Louisiana-style hot sauce
2 teaspoons salt
Several dashes Worcestershire sauce,
   optional
Yogurt or sour cream, for serving,
   optional

1 • *If using fresh corn,* steam or boil it for 3 to 5 minutes, or grill it (page 107). When it's cool enough to handle, cut a small slice off the fattest end of the corn. Stand the ear on the flat end in a bowl and, using a sharp knife, cut the corn off the cob. You should have about a cup of kernels. Set aside.

*If using frozen corn,* cook it according to the package directions. Drain well and set aside.

2 • Put the onion and garlic in the work bowl of a food processor and pulse until finely chopped. Add the bell peppers and jalapeño peppers and pulse until finely chopped. Add the tomatoes and pulse until soupy. Add the vinegar, chopped cilantro, sugar, hot sauce, salt, and Worcestershire sauce (if using) and pulse until well blended. The soup

will have plenty of texture but it shouldn't have any big lumps. (You can also make this in a blender, working in batches, using about $1/3$ of each ingredient per batch. Stir the 3 pureed batches together.)

3 • Transfer to a bowl, cover, and refrigerate until thoroughly chilled, at least 3 hours and up to 24 hours. Taste and add more vinegar, hot sauce, salt, sugar, or Worcestershire sauce, if needed.

4 • Garnish with whole cilantro leaves and serve with plain yogurt or sour cream on the side, if desired, or with a dollop of Guacamole (page 19) in the center.

*Makes about 6 cups, or 8 servings*

# Grilled Quesadillas

Sometimes it's hard to find something your kids will like other than burgers and hot dogs at a barbecue. Here's an item that kids and adults both like and is easy to get going while you're waiting to grill the main event.

---

*4 (10-inch) flour tortillas*
*8 ounces shredded Monterey Jack or*
  *cheddar cheese (about 2 cups)*

*Freshly ground pepper*

---

1 • Prepare a charcoal fire or preheat a gas grill for direct grilling over medium heat (see pages 11–14).

2 • Lay the tortillas on a flat work surface. Sprinkle half of each tortilla with $1/2$ cup cheese and some pepper. You can add other fillings if you like (see page 31); divide them among the tortillas, distributing the ingredients evenly over the cheese. Fold the empty half of the tortilla over the filled portion.

3 • The tortillas are not sealed, so you need to be careful when you transfer them to the grill—use a wide burger flipper to do so. Grill for about 5 minutes total, turning over once (carefully) halfway through the cooking time.

4 • Cut each quesadilla into 4 wedges. Serve as is, or topped with Salsa (page 20), Guacamole (page 19), or Black Bean Dip (page 22).

*Makes 16 pieces, or 8 servings*

## Bells and Whistles

*Customize your quesadillas to suit your taste buds with any (or all!) of the following filling ideas:*

$1/2$ green bell pepper, stemmed, seeded, and chopped

$1/2$ red bell pepper, stemmed, seeded, and chopped

$1/2$ medium red onion, peeled and finely chopped

4 scallions, white and green parts chopped

1 jalapeño pepper, stemmed, seeded, and finely chopped

$1/4$ cup chopped cilantro leaves

1 ($2 1/4$-ounce) can sliced black olives, drained ($1/2$ cup)

# Spicy Wings

I was going to call these Buffalo Wings, but I got a nasty call from people who live in upstate New York. Something about being found floating in Lake Erie. Caution being the better part of valor, we're calling 'em Spicy Wings.

8 tablespoons (1 stick) unsalted butter
1/2 cup Louisiana-style hot sauce,
      plus extra for serving
1 tablespoon packed light brown sugar
1 tablespoon garlic powder
1 tablespoon onion powder

1 teaspoon chili powder
1/2 teaspoon freshly ground pepper
1/4 teaspoon salt
4 pounds chicken wings (about
      18 wings)

1 • In a small saucepan set over medium heat, melt the butter. Reduce the heat to low, add all of the ingredients except for the chicken wings, and cook, stirring occasionally, for about 10 minutes, until the mixture is well blended and bubbling slightly. Remove the marinade from the heat and let cool to room temperature.

2 • Rinse the wings and pat them dry. Put them in a bowl, add the marinade, and toss to coat. Cover with plastic wrap and refrigerate for at least 4 hours and up to 8.

3 • When ready to cook, prepare a charcoal fire or preheat a gas grill for direct cooking over medium heat (see pages 11–14).

4 • Remove the wings from the bowl, and discard the marinade.

5 • Grill the wings for 25 to 35 minutes, turning once, until very crispy. Serve with extra hot sauce on the side.

*Makes 6 servings*

# The Main Attraction

# Your Basic Burger

Here's where we start talking about serious grilling. If you can't do the basics, then you shouldn't be doing fancy stuff. Think of it like driving. You learn on a Chevy Chevette before you step up to a Corvette. Burgers are not as easy as they look. Start with meat that has some fat (read: flavor) with 80% to 85% lean ground beef. Your butcher will be your best friend. Even if you're going to your local chain supermarket, the men and women behind the glass window will jump at the chance to do something for someone who respects the power of red meat on a grill. And for goodness sakes, don't keep moving the burger around. Let it sit there until it's time to flip it. And *do not,* I repeat, *do not* press the burger down with your spatula. All you do is squeeze out the natural juices of the meat and you're left with a dry lump of ground beef. Yuck!

2 pounds (80% to 85% lean)
   ground beef
1 tablespoon Worcestershire sauce
1 teaspoon coarse salt, such as
   kosher salt

1/2 teaspoon freshly ground pepper
12 (1-ounce) slices American, cheddar,
   Monterey Jack, or other cheese,
   optional
6 hamburger buns

1 • Prepare a charcoal fire or preheat a gas grill for direct grilling over high heat (see pages 11–14).

2 • In a large bowl, mix together the beef, Worcestershire sauce, salt, and pepper. Form into 6 patties, each approximately 5 ounces.

3 • Grill for 6 minutes, then turn over and, if using cheese, add 2 slices to each burger. Grill for 6 to 9 minutes more, until an instant-read thermometer inserted into the center of each burger reaches at least 160 degrees F. The burgers will be medium. During the last 1 to 2 minutes of grilling, put the buns on the grill, cut side down, and toast lightly.

4 • Transfer the hamburgers to the buns and add the toppings of your choice (see page 36).

*Makes 6 servings*

## Bells and Whistles

Salsa, store-bought or homemade (page 20)

Guacamole (page 19)

Black Bean Dip (page 22)

Grilled mushrooms (page 109)

Grilled onions (page 109)

Ketchup

Mustard

Sliced pickles

Lettuce

Sliced tomatoes

Crisp bacon

# Fancy Burgers

Follow the recipe for Your Basic Burger (page 35), but refrigerate the burger mixtures for at least 1 hour for the flavors to blend. Note that because these variations all contain ground pork, they should be grilled until an instant-read thermometer inserted in the center registers at least 165 degrees F.

## BBQ BURGERS

| | |
|---|---|
| 1 pound (80% to 85% lean) ground beef | 3 tablespoons BBQ Rub (page 174) |
| 1 pound ground pork | 4 teaspoons BBQ sauce (pages 184–187) |

## JERK BURGERS

No, this is not a burger named after your brother-in-law. It's named after the spice mix that flavors a lot of Caribbean cooking, as in jerk chicken or jerk pork.

| | |
|---|---|
| 1 pound ground turkey or chicken | 3 tablespoons Jerk Seasoning (page 176) |
| 1 pound ground pork | |

## ASIAN BURGERS

I'm a big fan of Asian cooking. I submitted my recipe for Pork Sashimi, but they rejected it, so we'll have to go with this.

| | |
|---|---|
| 1 pound ground turkey | 2 teaspoons peeled, minced fresh ginger |
| 1 pound ground pork | 2 teaspoons dry sherry |
| 2 scallions, white and green parts chopped | 1½ tablespoons soy sauce |
| 2 cloves garlic, peeled and minced | 1½ teaspoons Asian sesame oil |

# Not Your Usual Burger

I think every cookbook should have at least one weird recipe in it. Here's ours. My recipe buddy Marialisa swears by this. Where did she find it? At a local Romanian barbecue joint, of course. Isn't there one in your town?

| | |
|---|---|
| 2 pounds (80% to 85% lean) ground beef | 1/2 teaspoon freshly ground pepper |
| 1/2 cup low-sodium beef broth | 1/2 teaspoon ground allspice |
| 4 cloves garlic, peeled and minced | 1/4 teaspoon ground cloves |
| 1 teaspoon salt | 1/4 teaspoon dried thyme |
| | 1/4 teaspoon baking soda |

1 • Mix all of the ingredients together in a large bowl. Cover with plastic wrap and refrigerate for at least 24 hours, and up to 48 hours, for the flavors to blend.

2 • Prepare a charcoal fire or preheat a gas grill for direct grilling over high heat (see pages 11–14).

3 • Form the meat into 16 "sausages," each about 3 1/2 inches long, 2 inches wide, and 1 inch thick.

4 • Grill for 10 to 15 minutes, turning so that all sides are well browned. An instant-read thermometer inserted into the center of the patties should read at least 160 degrees F. The patties will be medium. Serve immediately.

*Makes 8 servings*

# Vegetarian Burgers

I'm a big fan of portobello mushroom burgers. They are simplicity unto themselves. Clean the mushrooms, snap off the stems, slather 'em with oil on both sides, and toss 'em on the grill. A few minutes on each side and you've got a "meaty"-tasting vegetarian burger. However, if you'd like something a little fancier, well, have we got a recipe for you!

4 large portobello mushrooms
2 tablespoons extra-virgin olive oil
Salt
Freshly ground pepper
2 large red bell peppers (see Note)
8 large slices crusty bread, preferably
   sourdough

4 ounces herbed cheese spread, or fresh
   goat cheese
12 large spinach leaves, stemmed,
   rinsed, and dried

1 • Prepare a charcoal fire or preheat a gas grill for direct grilling so that you have a medium-heat and a high-heat area (see pages 11–14).

2 • While the grill is heating, stem the mushrooms. You can leave the dark gills on the underside; they give the mushrooms a more intense flavor. If you choose to remove the gills, use the edge of a teaspoon to scoop them out. Wipe the mushrooms clean with a damp paper towel. Using a pastry brush, generously coat both sides of each mushroom with olive oil, and season with salt and pepper. Set the mushrooms aside.

3 • Put the whole peppers on the high-heat area of the grill, and roast, turning frequently, until the skin over almost all of the peppers turns black, about 20 minutes. Using tongs, remove the peppers from the grill, and place them in a heavy-duty, sealable plastic bag. Close the bag, and allow the peppers to cool somewhat.

4 • When they're cool enough to handle, remove the charred skin from the peppers and discard. Stem and seed the peppers, and cut each into 4 pieces.

5 • Grill the mushrooms over medium heat for about 15 minutes, turning once, until they are well browned and softened.

6 • While the mushrooms are grilling, toast the bread lightly over the high-heat area of the

grill, about 1 minute per side. Remove the bread from the grill and spread about 1 tablespoon of the cheese over each slice.

7 • Using tongs, remove a mushroom from the grill and place it on a piece of bread spread with cheese. Top with 2 pieces of the red pepper and 3 spinach leaves, then place a second piece of bread, cheese side down, on top. Repeat with the remaining ingredients, until you have made 4 sandwiches.

**NOTE:** You may substitute 1 (8-ounce) jar of roasted red peppers, drained, for the fresh peppers, and skip the roasting step.

*Makes 4 servings*

# Hot Dogs

Having grown up in New York City, I am used to the boiled hot dog available at most hot dog stands on the street and at Yankee Stadium. I also grew up eating my share of incinerated tube steaks at backyard barbecues both at home and away. That said, you've gotta love the hot dog. It's a perfect package. Meat and bread, all together. Kids and adults agree on loving hot dogs. How great is it when you're at a frou-frou cocktail party and you see a waiter with weenies in a blanket? That, my friend, is living!

According to the National Hot Dog and Sausage Council (www.hotdog.org), Americans buy about 9 billion hot dogs at the grocery store every year, which leads me to believe that most people are pretty confident about cooking them. Nevertheless, here are some helpful hints and a "recipe." If you can, buy knockwurst, which are thicker than most hot dogs and made of smoked pork or beef.

*8 thick hot dogs or knockwurst*
*8 hot dog buns*

1 • Prepare a charcoal fire or preheat a gas grill for direct grilling over high heat (see pages 11–14).

2 • Pierce each hot dog several times with the tines of a fork. Place on the grill and cook, turning each hot dog on all sides for about 8 minutes, or until nicely browned.

3 • During the last 1 to 2 minutes of grilling, lay the buns on the grill, cut side down, and toast lightly.

4 • Serve with the toppings of your choice (see page 43).

*Makes 8 servings*

## Puttin' on the Dog

**The Everything Dog:** Top with mustard, ketchup, chopped onions, sweet pickle relish, and sauerkraut.

**The Fiesta Dog:** Top with Salsa (page 20), finely chopped jalapeño peppers, sliced olives, and grated cheese.

**The Southwestern Dog:** Top with Corn, Black Bean, and Tomato Salad (page 98) and chipotle chiles (smoked jalapeño peppers).

**The Asian Dog:** Top with ketchup, hoisin sauce, chopped scallions, and bean sprouts.

**The Italian Dog:** Top with chopped tomatoes, grilled onions, and grilled bell peppers (page 110).

**The BBQ Dog:** Top with warm BBQ sauce (pages 184–187), chopped onions, chopped bell peppers, and hot sauce. Serve on white bread.

**The Campfire Dog:** Top with mustard, ketchup, and Best Baked Beans (page 94).

## STEAK 101

Steak is like TV. How many times have you heard someone say, "I never watch TV"? You know this is a person who secretly watches *Baywatch.* It's the same with steak. People who "never eat steak" will toss carnivore caution to the wind and take down half a pound of steak once the fat starts to sizzle on the grill! Always buy more steak than you need.

A little oil, salt, and pepper is about all you need for a great grilled steak; for a treat, finish each serving with a pat of Rosemary Butter (page 183). Tougher cuts will benefit from a marinade (pages 166–173).

### *Grades of Beef*

USDA PRIME designates beef that is well marbled with fat and therefore tastier and
   more tender than other grades. It is hard to find, as most is sold to restaurants and
   hotels. Ask at the meat counter.

USDA CHOICE designates beef that is moderately marbled and comes from fairly young
   cattle. It is widely available and a good choice for grilling.

USDA SELECT designates beef with small amounts of marbling and is therefore tougher
   and stringier. Try to avoid it for grilling, but if you do buy some, bring on the marinades to flavor and tenderize.

## Cuts of Beef

**PORTERHOUSE:** When I talk about "Steaks As Big As Your Head" (page 47), I usually mean porterhouse, a cut that combines a meaty strip and a tenderloin in one thick (1- to 2-inch) steak. One porterhouse (1½ to 2 pounds, including the bone) will feed 2 to 3 people.

**T-BONE:** Like a porterhouse but more tender, smaller, and thinner. Serve a steak (about 12 ounces each, including the bone) per person.

**RIB EYE (Delmonico):** My personal favorite cut of steak to grill. Ask your butcher to cut the steaks 2 inches or so thick. These are generously marbled with the secret ingredient . . . FAT, which makes them juicy and flavorful. A very forgiving steak, it is hard to overcook. You'll never forgive yourself if you don't try grilling this cut of beef.

**FILET MIGNON:** Tender as can be but a little bland. Not my #1 choice for the grill.

**STRIP STEAK (New York strip, top loin):** Lean and meaty, it can also be a bit stringy—a marinade will work wonders.

**FLANK STEAK (also incorrectly called "London Broil," which refers to the grilling method on page 48, not the cut):** Flavorful but tough, this steak—along with skirt steak—needs a long bath in an acidic marinade (pages 166–173) to tenderize it. To maximize tenderness, thinly slice the cooked steak at a 45-degree angle against the grain.

## Leftovers

-----------------------------------------------------------------------------------

*If you are lucky enough to have any leftover steak, you can use it in a variety of ways:*

**Steak Sandwich:** Place $1/4$ pound sliced steak on a piece of sourdough French or Italian bread or on a hard roll. Layer with Romaine or iceberg lettuce, sliced tomatoes, salt, pepper, and blue cheese dressing. Top with a second slice of bread or the other half of the roll.

**Philly Cheesesteak Pizza:** Stretch or roll out a pound of pizza dough to form a 12-inch circle. Top with $1/2$ to $3/4$ pound sliced steak, and 2 sautéed, thinly sliced onions. Top with 2 cups (8 ounces) shredded cheddar cheese and a few dashes of hot sauce. Bake at 425 degrees F for 15 to 20 minutes, until the cheese is bubbly and beginning to brown. Let sit for 5 minutes before slicing.

**Fajitas:** Sauté about $3/4$ pound leftover steak with 1 sliced onion and 1 sliced bell pepper. Divide among 4 heated, small (7-inch), flour tortillas and top with chopped fresh cilantro, finely chopped jalapeño peppers, chopped tomatoes, Salsa (page 20), Guacamole (page 19), or sour cream. Roll and serve.

Shrimp with
Cilantro-Mint Pesto (page 85)

*Grilled Quesadillas (page 30) with Guacamole (page 19)*

*Basic BBQ Chicken (page 54)*

*Steak Lover's Salad (page 49)*

Salmon with Maple-Ginger Glaze (page 82)

*Fish Fillets with Lemon-Parsley Sauce (page 80)*

*Summertime Green Bean Salad (page 116)*

*Corn, Black Bean, and Tomato Salad (page 98)*

*Kansas City–Style Ribs (page 66)*

Grilled Ham Steak with Drunken Peaches (page 73)

*London Broil (page 48) with Chile-Olive Dip (page 23)*

*Grilled fruit with Honey Glaze (page 126)*

*Lemon-Lime Fizz (page 159) and Pretty Pink Punch (page 158)*

*Mango-Melon-Berry Salad (page 128)*

*Peanut Butter–Chocolate Chip Cookie Ice Cream Sandwiches (page 146)*

# Steaks As Big As Your Head

2 porterhouse steaks, each about 1³/₄
    pounds and 1¹/₂ inches thick, or
    4 T-bone steaks, each about
    12 ounces and 1 inch thick, or other
    cut of your choice (page 45)
4 cloves garlic, peeled and cut into
    slivers
1¹/₂ cups extra-virgin olive oil

2 tablespoons chopped fresh rosemary
    leaves, or 1 tablespoon dried
    rosemary
Coarse salt, such as kosher salt
Freshly ground pepper
¹/₂ recipe Rosemary Butter (page 183),
    at room temperature, optional

1 • Rinse the steak under cold running water and pat dry with paper towels. With a sharp knife, make several small cuts in the meat, without cutting all the way through. Press a sliver of garlic into each cut. If you have any garlic left over, set it aside.

2 • In a shallow, non-reactive pan, mix together the olive oil, rosemary, salt, pepper, and any leftover slivers of garlic.

3 • Place the steak in the olive oil marinade and turn to coat. Let sit at room temperature for about 30 minutes.

4 • Meanwhile, prepare a charcoal fire or preheat a gas grill for direct grilling over high heat (see pages 11–14).

5 • Remove the steaks from the pan, discard the marinade, and place the steaks on the grill. A thicker steak (such as the porterhouse) will take at least 10 minutes per side to reach medium-rare (145 degrees F on an instant-read thermometer) and a thinner steak (such as the T-bone) will take as little as 7 minutes per side.

6 • Remove the steak from the grill and place it on a cutting board. Cover the meat with a piece of aluminum foil to keep it warm, and allow the meat to rest for 5 minutes. Cut the meat off the bone, and slice it against the grain. Top each serving with 1 or 2 pats of rosemary butter, if desired.

*Makes 4 servings*

# London Broil

Recommended marinades include Asian Marinade (page 166), Southwestern Marinade (page 167), and Red Wine Marinade (page 168).

*3 pounds flank steak (or chuck shoulder, top round, or bottom round)*
*Marinade of your choice (pages 166–173)*

1 • Rinse the meat under cold running water and pat dry with paper towels. Place the meat in a shallow, non-reactive pan, and pour the marinade over the meat. Turn to coat. Cover with plastic wrap and refrigerate for at least 8 hours, or up to 24, turning the meat once during this time. Let sit at room temperature for about 30 minutes before grilling.

2 • Prepare a charcoal fire or preheat a gas grill for direct grilling over high heat (see pages 11–14).

3 • Remove the steaks from the pan and discard the marinade. Grill the steaks until done to your liking; an instant-read thermometer inserted into the thickest part of the meat should read at least 145 degrees F for medium-rare, 160 degrees F for medium. It will take 6 to 8 minutes on each side to reach medium-rare.

4 • Remove the meat from the grill and place it on a cutting board. Cover the meat with a piece of aluminum foil to keep it warm, and allow the meat to rest for 5 minutes before slicing.

5 • Slice the meat thinly at a 45-degree angle against the grain (otherwise it will be tough). Serve immediately.

*Makes 6 servings*

# Steak Lover's Salad

I came up with this recipe quite by accident. One Saturday, I was taking the steak out of the fridge when Deborah said, "I hope we're having something healthy for dinner!" I looked at the red meat in my hand and thought, "Uh-oh."

I dove back into the icebox and pulled out some greens, tomatoes, a left-over Vidalia onion, and some store-bought dressing. After grilling the steak, I sliced it up, and settled it on top of the greens. I threw on some crumbled blue cheese for good measure, and *voilà!*

Deborah looked at my creation and said, "You're not fooling anybody, buster!" That said, her plate was clean as a whistle at the end of dinner.

---

12 cups mixed salad greens, rinsed,
    dried, and cut into bite-sized pieces
    (see Note)
6 medium tomatoes, stemmed and
    thinly sliced
2 medium cucumbers, peeled and
    thinly sliced
1 medium Vidalia or red onion, peeled
    and thinly sliced

London Broil (page 48), preferably
    made with Red Wine Marinade
    (page 168)
1/2 pound blue cheese
Basic Vinaigrette (page 181), made
    with Dijon mustard

---

1 • Divide the greens, tomatoes, cucumbers, and onion among 6 plates.

2 • Slice the London Broil thinly at a 45-degree angle against the grain (otherwise it will be tough), and divide the meat among the serving plates, placing it directly on top of the greens. Sprinkle some blue cheese over the steak, and drizzle with the vinaigrette (you may not need all of it; extra dressing can be kept, covered and refrigerated, for up to 2 days). Serve immediately.

**NOTE:** You want to use crisp lettuce, such as Romaine, for the bulk of the greens; mix it with a bit of a softer lettuce such as Boston or red-leaf, and a strong-flavored green such as arugula or watercress.

*Makes 6 servings*

# Essential Beef Brisket

Like ribs (pages 66–69) and Pulled Pork (page 70), brisket is a test of the barbecue-meister's patience and skill. The trick is long, slow grilling over low heat and basting with the mop of your choice.

---

1 (5- to 6-pound) brisket
Beef Rub (page 175)
Beer Mop (page 177) or Wine Mop
   (page 178)

About 5 cups wood chips

---

1 • Rinse the meat under cold running water and pat dry with paper towels. Pat the rub all over the brisket on both sides, rubbing it in with your hands. Cover with plastic wrap and refrigerate for at least 8 hours and up to 24 hours. Let sit at room temperature for about 30 minutes before grilling.

2 • Soak the wood chips (hickory, oak, or apple) for at least 30 minutes in cold water (see page 7).

3 • Prepare a charcoal fire or preheat a gas grill for indirect grilling over low heat (see pages 11–14). Drain the wood chips and add 1 cup to the grill.

4 • Put the brisket, fat side up, in a disposable aluminum pan on the grill. Using a barbecue mop (page 9), a pastry brush, or a long-handled spoon, coat the meat with the beer or wine mop.

5 • Grill, covered, basting with the mop every hour, and turning once, until an instant-read thermometer inserted into the thickest part of the meat reads 190 degrees F. This will take $4^1/_2$ to 6 hours, depending on the size of the brisket and the heat of your grill. Don't forget to add more wood chips—and, if using charcoal, more coals—as needed (check every hour or so). You should have enough soaked wood chips for about 5 hours of cooking time; if the brisket takes longer, you will need to soak more chips.

6 • Remove the brisket from the grill and place it on a cutting board. Cover the meat with a piece of aluminum foil to keep it warm and allow it to rest for 5 minutes before slicing. Slice the meat thinly at a 45-degree angle against the grain (otherwise it will be tough). Serve with the pan juices poured on top.

*Makes 10 to 12 servings*

# Korean Barbecued Short Ribs

Serve with rice and Asian Slaw (page 114). Also good with kimchi (pickled cabbage, available in Asian markets and some supermarkets). Just know that kimchi can be pretty spicy, and when combined with baked beans can make for an uncomfortable night in the absence of *goood* ventilation, if you get my drift!

---

*1/2 cup peanut oil*
*1/2 cup rice vinegar*
*1/4 cup soy sauce*
*4 cloves garlic, peeled and minced*
*2 tablespoons ketchup*
*1 tablespoon hot Asian chili paste*
     *(available in supermarkets)*

*1 tablespoon sesame seeds, optional*
*2 teaspoons Asian sesame oil*
*6 pounds beef short ribs, cut 1/4 to 1/2*
     *inch thick, crosswise through a rack*
     *of 4 ribs (ask the butcher to*
     *do this)*

---

1 • In a non-reactive pan or bowl just large enough to hold the meat, mix together all of the ingredients except the short ribs.

2 • Toss the meat gently in the pan until lightly coated. Cover with plastic wrap and refrigerate for at least 8 hours and up to 24, turning the meat gently once during this time.

3 • Prepare a charcoal fire or preheat a gas grill for direct grilling over high heat (see pages 11–14).

4 • Remove the ribs from the pan and discard the marinade. Grill the meat until well browned and crispy on the outside, about 5 minutes per side. Serve immediately.

*Makes 6 servings*

# Poultry 101

When I am really trying to eat a little "lighter" *and* I'm in a hurry, nothing beats Grilled Chicken Breasts (page 55).

But don't forget that there are other parts of a chicken as well. Packages of thighs, legs, and wings make good, economical eating, and most of the marinades and rubs—which tenderize and add flavor—can be used interchangeably for all parts. Generally, remember that bone-in pieces take longer to cook than boneless, and dark meat takes longer than white. Cook bone-in pieces covered, over indirect heat, and boneless pieces over direct heat.

*To grill a whole (3$^1/_2$- to 4-pound) chicken,* remove the giblets from the cavity, rinse the chicken inside and out under cold running water, and pat dry with paper towels. If the chicken has a pop-up thermometer, remove it. Rub the chicken all over with oil or softened butter, season it as you like (try one of the rubs on pages 174–175), then grill it, covered, over indirect, medium heat (see pages 11–14) until the juices run clear when the thigh meat is pierced, and an instant-read thermometer inserted in the thickest part of the thigh reads 180 degrees F. This will take 1$^1/_4$ to 1$^3/_4$ hours, depending on the size of the chicken and the heat of your grill.

*To grill a half chicken,* follow the same method as above, grilling it, covered, skin side up over indirect medium heat (see pages 11–14) for about 1 hour, or until the juices run clear when the thigh meat is pierced, and an instant-read thermometer inserted in the thickest part of the thigh reads 180 degrees F. Do not turn the chicken while grilling. When done, flip it over, skin side down, over direct high heat, and grill for 5 to 10 minutes, until the skin is crispy.

## Leftovers

**"Pulled" Chicken:** Shred leftover Basic BBQ Chicken (page 54) and warm it in a saucepan with enough BBQ sauce (see pages 184–187) to moisten it well. Serve on white bread or rolls. You can also serve the pulled chicken with extra BBQ sauce over cooked spaghetti.

**Chicken Salad:** Add diced, leftover chicken to Corn, Black Bean, and Tomato Salad (page 98) or to Pasta Salad with Parmesan and Basil (page 104) for a light lunch or supper.

**Fajitas:** Cut $3/4$ pound leftover chicken into strips, and sauté with 1 sliced onion and 1 sliced bell pepper. Divide among 4 heated, small (7-inch), flour tortillas and top with chopped cilantro leaves, finely chopped jalapeño peppers, chopped tomatoes, Salsa (page 20), Guacamole (page 19), Black Bean Dip (page 22), or sour cream. Roll and serve.

# Basic BBQ Chicken

Is there anything that says summer and backyard barbecue more than BBQ chicken? Here's where a good barbecue sauce comes in handy. Let's face it; chicken is a rather bland protein. You never hear anyone say, "It tastes too chicken-y," do you?

That's why good BBQ chicken calls out for good seasoning and great BBQ sauce. We have provided both!

| | |
|---|---|
| 1 (3½- to 4-pound) chicken, cut into 8 pieces | ⅓ cup BBQ Rub (page 174) |
| | 3 cups BBQ sauce (pages 184–187) |

1 • Rinse the chicken under cold running water and pat dry with paper towels. Sprinkle the rub all over the chicken, rubbing it in with your fingers. Cover with plastic wrap and refrigerate for at least 2 hours and up to 12 hours. Let sit at room temperature for 20 minutes before grilling.

2 • Prepare a charcoal fire or preheat a gas grill for indirect grilling over medium heat (see pages 11–14).

3 • Put the thighs and legs on the grill, cover, and, 10 minutes later, add the chicken breasts and wings, to allow for different grilling times. Grill the chicken, turning once, for about 45 minutes. Pour about 1 cup BBQ sauce into a small bowl and baste the chicken with it, using a barbecue mop (page 9), a pastry brush, or a long-handled spoon, while you are grilling.

4 • Grill until the juices run clear when the thigh meat is pierced and an instant-read thermometer inserted in the thickest part of the thigh reads 180 degrees F. This will take 1 to 1½ hours total. Discard any remaining BBQ sauce in the bowl.

5 • Remove the chicken from the grill and place it on a cutting board. Cover the chicken with a piece of aluminum foil to keep it warm, and allow the chicken to rest for 5 minutes before serving. Heat the remaining 2 cups of BBQ sauce and serve on the side.

*Makes 4 servings*

# Grilled Chicken Breasts, Any Way, Any Day

Boneless, skinless chicken breasts rank high on the list of today's "convenience foods" and are a snap to grill. They are also versatile. A stand-alone main course, chicken breasts slip into a bun quite nicely in place of a burger or can be sliced after grilling to replace the steak in my Steak Lover's Salad (page 49). Try the Tandoori Rub and Marinade (page 173), Orange-Rosemary Marinade (page 169), White Wine–Tarragon Marinade (page 171), or Honey-Mustard Marinade (page 170).

*6 (6-ounce) boneless, skinless chicken breast halves*
*Marinade of your choice (pages 166–173)*

1 • Rinse the chicken under cold running water and pat dry with paper towels. Put the chicken pieces in a shallow, non-reactive pan and pour the marinade over the chicken. Turn each piece to coat. Cover and refrigerate for at least 4 hours, or up to 12 hours, turning once during this time. Let sit at room temperature for 20 minutes before grilling.

2 • Prepare a charcoal fire or preheat a gas grill for direct grilling over medium heat (see pages 11–14).

3 • Remove the chicken from the pan and discard the marinade. Grill the chicken for 6 to 8 minutes per side, until the outside is well browned, the meat is no longer pink when pierced, and an instant-read thermometer inserted into the center reads 170 degrees F. Serve immediately.

*Makes 6 servings*

# Chicken Caesar Salad
# with Grilled Croutons

There have been times, while dining at a restaurant, I've come across an offering on the menu that drives me nuts: "Grilled Chicken Caesar Salad." Call me a purist, but once you add grilled chicken to the Caesar salad, it's no longer a Caesar salad. It's a salad with grilled chicken!

Deborah says I need to get over myself and enjoy the salad. It doesn't really matter what it's called. It's *goood.* So I've gotten over myself!

---

6 (6-ounce) boneless, skinless chicken
    breast halves
Caesar Dressing (page 182)
1$^1$/$_2$ heads Romaine lettuce, leaves
    washed and drained
$^1$/$_2$ large red onion, peeled and finely
    chopped

12 slices day-old crusty bread
$^1$/$_3$ cup extra-virgin olive oil
2 cloves garlic, peeled and halved
Freshly ground pepper
Small chunk of Parmesan cheese,
    optional

---

1 • Rinse the chicken under cold running water and pat dry with paper towels. Put the chicken in a shallow, non-reactive pan and pour $^3$/$_4$ cup of the dressing over the chicken. Turn to coat. The chicken should just be coated, not swimming in marinade. Pour the remaining dressing into a bowl, cover, and refrigerate until ready to use. Cover the chicken with plastic wrap and refrigerate for at least 4 hours and up to 12 hours. Let sit at room temperature for 20 minutes before grilling.

2 • Prepare a charcoal fire or preheat a gas grill for direct grilling over medium heat (see pages 11–14).

3 • While the grill is heating, prepare the salad plates. Tear the lettuce into bite-sized pieces and divide among 6 plates. Divide the onion among the plates, sprinkling it over the lettuce.

4 • Using a pastry brush, coat both sides of each slice of bread with the olive oil. Grill the bread for 1 to 2 minutes on each side, until well toasted. Rub both sides of each toasted

slice with the cut side of a garlic clove. Cut each slice of bread into bite-sized cubes and set aside. Discard the garlic.

5 • Remove the chicken from the pan and discard the marinade. Grill the chicken for 6 to 8 minutes per side, until the outside is well browned, the meat is no longer pink when pierced, and an instant-read thermometer inserted into the center reads 170 degrees F.

6 • Slice the breasts and place the slices on the salad on each plate. Top with the croutons and then drizzle with the remaining ³/₄ cup of dressing. Grind some pepper over each plate. Use a vegetable peeler to shave thin curls of Parmesan cheese over each plate, if desired, then serve.

*Makes 6 servings*

# Beer Can Chicken

I know that I am in the minority here (no pun intended) when I tell you that I do not drink beer. I know you're thinking, "Al, you look like that and you don't take a pull on a long, tall cold one every now and again?" I hate to disappoint, but the answer is no. Never developed a taste for it. Consequently, I've always felt like I'm missing out on part of the barbecue/grilling experience. Of course, occasionally I'm at a backyard barbecue when I see my host go face-down in the guacamole after a six-pack or two, and I think, "There, but for the grace of God and Deborah . . ."

That said, I feel it is my responsibility, nay, my duty, to include the following recipe.

---

1 (5- to 6-pound) chicken
2 tablespoons BBQ Rub (page 174)

1 (12-ounce) can beer

---

1 • Prepare a charcoal fire or preheat a gas grill for indirect grilling over medium heat (see pages 11–14).

2 • Remove the giblets from the chicken and rinse the chicken, inside and out, under cold running water. Pat dry with paper towels. If the chicken has a pop-up thermometer, remove it. Sprinkle the chicken, inside and out, with the rub.

3 • Open the can of beer and pour out half ($^3/_4$ cup). What you do with that $^3/_4$ cup of beer is your business. Set the open can on a flat work surface and slide the chicken over the top of the can so that the can fits snugly in the cavity of the chicken. Carefully transfer the chicken to the grill, balancing it on the tripod made by its legs and the beer can.

4 • Grill, covered, until the juices run clear when the thigh meat is pierced and an instant-read thermometer inserted in the thickest part of the thigh reads 180 degrees F. This will take $1^1/_4$ to $1^3/_4$ hours, depending on the size of the chicken and the heat of your grill.

5 • Remove the chicken—with the can—from the grill and place on a flat work surface.

Remove the can and discard any remaining beer. Cover the chicken with a large piece of aluminum foil to keep it warm, and allow the chicken to rest for about 5 minutes before carving. Carve the chicken and serve.

*Makes 4 servings*

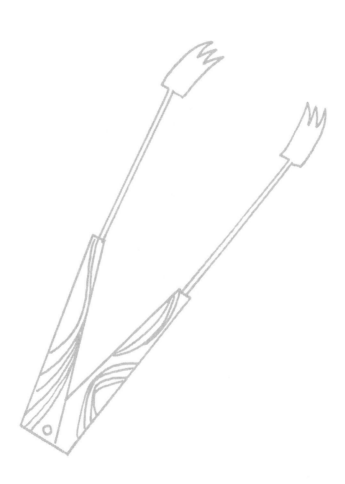

# Jerk Chicken

This is not a recipe named after your boss. The word "jerk" refers to the spice mixture used to coat the chicken. Brought to Jamaica and other Caribbean climes by African slaves, jerk has been used to season pork, chicken, and anything else running around the backyard.

1 (3½- to 4-pound) chicken, cut into 8 pieces
Jerk Seasoning (page 176)

1 • Rinse the chicken pieces under cold running water and pat dry with paper towels. Rub the chicken pieces all over with the jerk seasoning. Cover with plastic wrap and refrigerate for at least 4 hours and up to 12 hours. Let sit at room temperature for 20 minutes before grilling.

2 • Prepare a charcoal fire or preheat a gas grill for indirect grilling over medium heat (see pages 11–14).

3 • Put the thighs and legs on the grill, cover, and, 10 minutes later, add the chicken breasts and wings, to allow for different grilling times. Grill the chicken, turning once, for 1 to 1½ hours, or until the juices run clear when the meat is pierced and the internal temperature reaches 180 degrees F in the thickest part of the thighs and 170 degrees F in the breasts.

4 • Serve with Tropical Fruit Salsa (page 93) and My Mom's Peas and Rice (page 96), if desired.

*Makes 4 servings*

# Turkey on the Grill

Turkey is one of those items that you almost never think of apart from Christmas and Thanksgiving. Yet it's as versatile as chicken; it just needs a little more help to be really enjoyable. A few years ago, I discovered the secret of brining. I found that it makes for a juicy, moist roast turkey as it does when grilling said bird. Brining is an extra step but well worth it. Once you brine your bird, you will never look at turkey the same way. Benjamin Franklin thought enough of the turkey to try to make it the national bird. Let's do justice to this noble fowl.

Put the turkey in a disposable aluminum pan while grilling so that you can baste the bird and capture the drippings to make a delicious, smoky gravy. The turkey, when done, will be a deep, rich, mahogany color.

## TO BRINE

*5 quarts water*
*1 cup coarse salt, such as kosher or*
*    sea salt*
*6 cloves garlic, smashed and peeled*
*5 bay leaves*

*2 tablespoons whole peppercorns*
*    (a mixture of colors—black, green,*
*    and pink—is nice, but not strictly*
*    necessary)*
*1 (12- to 14-pound) turkey*

1 • The night before you are going to grill, combine all of the ingredients except the turkey in a large pot set over high heat. Bring to a boil, reduce the heat to a simmer, and cook for 10 minutes. Remove the pot from the heat and cool the brine to room temperature.

2 • Remove the giblets from the turkey and rinse the turkey, inside and out, under cold running water. If the turkey has a pop-up thermometer, remove it. Immerse the turkey in the brine, either in the pot, a very large bowl, or a clean plastic bucket. You may need to place a weight on the turkey to keep it submerged; a clean brick wrapped in a sealable plastic bag or several layers of aluminum foil works well. Cover and refrigerate overnight.

1 orange, halved
1 lemon, halved
1 small onion, peeled and halved
Small bunch parsley sprigs
3 cloves garlic, smashed and peeled
2 bay leaves
8 tablespoons (1 stick) unsalted butter

About 2 cups low-sodium chicken broth
Water, apple cider, or white wine,
 optional
All-purpose flour

About 3 cups wood chips

1 • Soak the wood chips (hickory, oak, or apple) for at least 30 minutes in cold water (page 7).

2 • Prepare a charcoal fire or preheat a gas grill for indirect grilling over medium heat (see pages 11–14). Drain the wood chips and add 1 cup to the grill.

3 • Drain the turkey thoroughly and pat it dry with paper towels. Discard the brine. Put the turkey, breast side up, in a disposable aluminum roasting pan. Stuff the cavity with the orange, lemon, onion, parsley, garlic, and bay leaves. Rub the skin of the turkey all over with half of the butter. No need for salt and pepper—the brine has taken care of that.

4 • Put the turkey—in the pan—on the grill, and cover. After the first hour of grilling, heat the remaining 4 tablespoons of butter with 1 1/2 cups of the chicken broth. Baste the turkey with the broth, using a barbecue mop (page 9), a pastry brush, a long-handled spoon, or a turkey baster. Keep at it every hour or so, using the juices in the pan for basting. If the drumsticks or breasts begin to brown too quickly, cover them with heavy-duty aluminum foil.

5 • Don't forget to add more wood chips—and, if using charcoal, more coals—as needed (check every hour or so). You should have enough soaked wood chips for about 3 hours of cooking time; if your turkey takes longer, you will need to soak more chips.

6 • If the temperature is kept steady at medium heat (300 to 350 degrees F), the pan drippings should not burn. If they look like they are burning, add a bit of water, apple cider, or white wine to the pan.

7 • Cook the turkey until the juices run clear when the thigh meat is pierced and an instant-read thermometer inserted into the thickest part of the thigh reaches 180 degrees F. (The drumstick will be very wiggly.) This will take 3 to 4 hours, depending on the size of your turkey and the heat of your grill.

8 • Remove the turkey from the grill and place it on a cutting board. Cover the turkey with a large piece of aluminum foil to keep it warm, and allow the turkey to rest for at least 10 minutes before slicing.

9 • While the turkey is resting, make the gravy. Pour the pan juices into a heatproof glass container (a quart measuring cup works well) and allow the fat to rise to the top. Skim off the fat, spooning it into a saucepan, and add an equal amount of flour. (In other words, if you have $1/4$ cup of fat, add $1/4$ cup of flour). Stir constantly over low heat, until the fat and flour form a thick, smooth paste. Add the juices that separated from the skimmed fat, and add some or all of the remaining $1/2$ cup of chicken broth until you have reached the desired consistency. Do not let the gravy boil.

10 • Carve the turkey and serve with the gravy on the side.

*Makes 12 servings*

# Barbecue!

## (*And my own secret formula*)

My father taught me never to get into an argument about religion or politics. He forgot to mention barbecue. A man will probably change his mind about what church he will worship in or who he will vote for before he will switch sides on what is the best kind of barbecue.

You see, almost every region of the country has taken barbecue and made it their own. The secret to the perfect barbecue might be the seasonings, or the type of sauce, or lack thereof. It can even be the kind or cut of meat. I know that in Texas, barbecued bologna alongside beef brisket is a big deal. And when it comes to barbecue sauce, the debate can rage for hours. Family recipes are closely guarded secrets; generations are sworn to secrecy. That's the kind of fanaticism that barbecue sauce generates.

I feel about barbecue sauce the same way I feel about steak sauce. If the meat is good quality and it's prepared well, sauce just covers up a good thing. It's like having a Picasso and spray painting over it. You can do it, but why?

I have included a few recipes here, but you wanna know what my secret recipe is? I grab a few bottles of whatever's on sale and add some honey mustard, a few spices—Hungarian paprika, ground allspice, cumin, and black pepper—and a little extra ketchup and that's about it. There is one sauce that I am pretty partial to, if I have to name one. It's called Jack's BBQ Sauce Cowboy Ketchup (see Sources, page 191). It's made by a guy named Jack (who would've guessed?) out in Indio, California. YUMMY!

The best part about barbecue is that it is slow cooked. In these times of rushing and getting things as fast as possible, you can't rush great ribs. Cooked slowly with indirect heat, they take on the flavor of the wood you use for smoke. Today, there are so many possibilities, ranging from hickory to apple wood and everything in between (see Wood Chips, page 7). We've included a couple of places to order wood in the source guide. Experiment. See what flavors are imparted. What's the worst that can happen? You've gotta make another batch of ribs. Boo-hoo . . . pass me another Wet-Nap.

# Kansas City–Style Ribs

These are called "wet" ribs because they are basted with BBQ sauce during the last few minutes of grilling and served with plenty of sauce on the side.

6 pounds spareribs
1 cup cider vinegar
1 cup apple cider
4 cloves garlic, peeled and minced
2 bay leaves
2 tablespoons Louisiana-style hot sauce
2 tablespoons salt

2 tablespoons chili powder
2 tablespoons garlic powder
3 cups favorite BBQ sauce (pages 184–187)

About 3 cups wood chips

1 • Your ribs may already be trimmed, or you can ask the butcher to trim them. To do it your-self, place the ribs meat side up on a cutting board. There is a line of fat at the base of the ribs; cut along it to remove the cartilaginous rib tips. Turn the meat over, rib side up. Cut off the flap of meat on the inside of the ribs. (The reason for removing these pieces is that they will burn well before the ribs are done. You can season them and grill them over direct heat for about 15 minutes, turning once. They are delicious.) With the rib side up, finesse a sharp knife under the tough membrane that covers the bones. Working from one rib to the next, pull the membrane off the rib. (For a better grip, grab the mem-brane with a paper towel.) The membrane may tear and you may have to start over, but be patient—removing the membrane allows the spices and smoke to penetrate the ribs, and makes the ribs much more attractive and easy to eat.

2 • In a shallow, non-reactive pan large enough to hold the ribs, mix together the cider vine-gar, cider, garlic, bay leaves, hot sauce, and 1 tablespoon of the salt. Put the ribs in this marinade, turn to coat, cover with plastic wrap, and refrigerate for at least 8 hours and up to 16 hours, turning once during this time.

3 • Two hours before you are going to grill, remove the ribs from the pan and pat them dry. Discard the marinade. Combine the chili powder, garlic powder, and the remaining table-spoon of salt and sprinkle over the ribs. Cover and refrigerate for about 1$^1$/$_2$ hours. Remove the ribs from the refrigerator and let sit at room temperature for 30 minutes before grilling.

4 • Soak the wood chips (hickory, oak, or apple) for at least 30 minutes in cold water (see page 7).

5 • Prepare a charcoal fire or preheat a gas grill for indirect grilling over low heat (see pages 11–14). Drain the wood chips and add 1 cup to the grill.

6 • Grill the ribs, covered, for 2 3/4 hours, turning the ribs once. Don't forget to add more wood chips—and, if using charcoal, more coals—as needed (check every hour or so).

7 • Pour 1 cup of BBQ sauce into a small bowl and, using a barbecue mop (page 9), a pastry brush, or a long-handled spoon, generously baste the ribs. Repeat at least once before you remove the ribs from the grill. Discard any sauce remaining in the basting bowl. The ribs are done when they are crispy, and the meat has pulled back from the bone. This will take 3 to 4 hours total, depending on the heat of your grill. You should have enough soaked wood chips for about 3 hours of cooking time; if your ribs take longer, you will need to soak more chips.

8 • If the ribs are done before you are ready to eat, wrap them in heavy-duty aluminum foil and leave them over very low, indirect heat for up to 1 hour.

9 • Heat the remaining 2 cups of BBQ sauce in a small saucepan set over low heat. Pour into a bowl and pass with the ribs.

*Makes 6 servings*

# Memphis-Style Ribs

These are my personal favorites. Memphis-style ribs are called "dry" ribs because they are crispy and chewy and grilled without any sauce. They are, however, sometimes served with sauce on the side—often vinegar sauce. Place it in small pitchers on the table for people to pour over the ribs. For those who have to have barbecue sauce, I put out a couple of pitchers of my doctored store-bought and fix the offending consumer of my ribs with a hard glare. Try 'em without sauce first. See what good ribs taste like without being covered up with a sweet tomato-y sauce.

6 pounds spareribs
1³/₄ cups cider vinegar
1³/₄ cups apple cider
4 cloves garlic, peeled and minced
2 bay leaves
3 tablespoons Louisiana-style hot sauce,
    such as Tabasco

1 tablespoon salt
³/₄ cup BBQ Rub (page 174)
Vinegar Sauce (page 187), optional

About 3 cups wood chips

1 • Your ribs may already be trimmed, or you can ask the butcher to trim them. To do it your-self, place the ribs meat side up on a cutting board. There is a line of fat at the base of the ribs; cut along it to remove the cartilaginous rib tips. Turn the meat over, rib side up. Cut off the flap of meat on the inside of the ribs. (The reason for removing these pieces is that they will burn well before the ribs are done. You can season them and grill them over direct heat for about 15 minutes, turning once. They are delicious.) With the rib side up, finesse a sharp knife under the tough membrane that covers the bones. Working from one rib to the next, pull the membrane off the rib. (For a better grip, grab the mem-brane with a paper towel.) The membrane may tear and you may have to start over, but be patient—removing the membrane allows the spices and smoke to penetrate the ribs and makes the ribs much more attractive and easy to eat.

2 • In a shallow, non-reactive pan large enough to hold the ribs, mix together 1 cup of the cider vinegar, 1 cup of the cider, the garlic, bay leaves, 2 tablespoons of the hot sauce,

and salt. Put the ribs in this marinade, turn to coat, cover with plastic wrap, and refrigerate for at least 8 hours and up to 16 hours, turning once during this time.

3 • Two hours before you are going to grill, remove the ribs from the pan and pat dry. Discard the marinade. Sprinkle the ribs all over with $1/2$ cup of the rub, patting it on with your fingers. Cover and refrigerate for about $1^1/_2$ hours. Remove the ribs from the refrigerator and let sit at room temperature for 30 minutes before grilling.

4 • Mix the remaining $3/4$ cup cider vinegar, $3/4$ cup cider, and 1 tablespoon hot sauce. You will apply this mixture to the ribs once every hour or so with a spray bottle, a barbecue mop (page 9), a pastry brush, or a long-handled spoon.

5 • Soak the wood chips (hickory, oak, or apple) for at least 30 minutes in cold water (see page 7).

6 • Prepare a charcoal fire or preheat a gas grill for indirect grilling over low heat (see pages 11–14). Drain the wood chips and add 1 cup to the grill.

7 • Grill the ribs, covered, until they are crispy, and the meat has pulled back from the bone, 3 to 4 hours, depending on the heat of your grill. Spray or baste the ribs with the vinegar-cider mixture every hour, and turn them once during grilling. Don't forget to add more wood chips—and, if using charcoal, more coals—as needed (check every hour or so). You should have enough soaked wood chips for about 3 hours of cooking time; if your ribs take longer, you will need to soak more chips.

8 • If the ribs are done before you are ready to eat, wrap them in heavy-duty aluminum foil and leave them over very low, indirect heat for up to 1 hour.

9 • Remove the ribs from the grill, spray or baste with any remaining basting liquid, and sprinkle with the remaining $1/4$ cup of rub. Serve as is or with vinegar sauce.

*Makes 6 servings*

# Pulled Pork

Oh, man. This is what barbecue is all about. The perfect summer meal when you've got family and friends over. It takes the better part of the day to make, so allow yourself at least 4 or 5 hours. If I have friends coming over about noon, I usually start my pork butt at about 7 A.M. That's why I have hot dogs and hamburgers at the ready. These are the appetizers to get you ready for the main event.

And let's face it, any time you can walk into your local grocery store and ask for "butt," it's the start of a good time. Best part about this is that pork butt is a pretty inexpensive cut of meat and you don't have to go to a fancy butcher shop to get it. I usually go into one of my local chain supermarkets and ring the butcher bell. Plus, it's neat to see the window slide open and talk to someone about ordering a butt. You obviously can tell . . . I'm a butt man.

Don't get fancy rolls or bread. Cheap buns (there's that butt thing again) and squishy white bread are the order of the day. They soak up all the juice from the pulled pork and absorb the sauce. Great with Collards (page 119), corn bread (pages 120–122), and Classic Cole Slaw (page 112). This, my friends, is good eating!

---

*5 pounds fresh (not smoked) pork butt, bone-in (look for the cut sold as Boston Butt)*
*⅓ cup BBQ Rub (page 174)*

*5 cups BBQ sauce (pages 184–187)*

*About 4 cups wood chips*

---

1 • Place the pork butt, fat side up, in a disposable aluminum roasting pan and sprinkle the rub all over it, making sure all sides are coated. You can grill it immediately, or you can cover it with plastic wrap and refrigerate it for up to 24 hours. This is preferable; the flavors will have time to soak in.

2 • Soak the wood chips (hickory, oak, or apple) for at least 30 minutes in cold water (see page 7).

3 • Prepare a charcoal fire or preheat a gas grill for indirect grilling over low heat (see pages 11–14). Drain the wood chips and add 1 cup to the grill.

4 • Put the pan on the grill, cover, and cook the pork, without turning, until the skin is crispy and an instant-read thermometer inserted in the thickest part of the meat reads 190 degrees F. This will take 4 to 5 hours, depending on the heat of your grill. Don't forget to add more wood chips—and, if using charcoal, more coals—as needed (check every hour or so). You should have enough soaked wood chips for about 4 hours of cooking time; if the pork takes longer, you will need to soak more chips.

5 • Remove the pork from the grill and place it on a cutting board. Allow the pork to cool enough so that you can handle it. Pull it apart with your hands, discarding bits of fat and the bone, and place the shredded meat in a bowl. Chop the crispy skin and add it to the pulled pork. (Try not to eat it all.)

6 • In a large saucepan, mix the pork with about 3 cups of BBQ sauce and warm slowly over medium heat until heated through. In a separate small saucepan, warm the remaining 2 cups of sauce.

7 • Serve the pork as is, or on white bread or a roll, with the extra BBQ sauce on the side.

*Makes 10 pulled pork sandwiches or 8 platter servings*

# Marinated Pork Tenderloin

Especially good with Caribbean Marinade (page 172) or Honey-Mustard Marinade (page 170). If using the Caribbean marinade, you may want to serve the pork with grilled pineapple (page 127), Tropical Fruit Salsa (page 93), and My Mom's Peas and Rice (page 96). Pork tenderloin is also good with grilled onions (page 109).

3 pounds pork tenderloin
Marinade of your choice (pages 166–173)

1 • The night before you are going to grill, use a very sharp knife to remove the silvery strip of skin from the tenderloin and discard. Put the pork in a shallow, non-reactive pan and pour the marinade over the meat. Cover and refrigerate for at least 8 hours and up to 24 hours, turning once during this time. Let the pork sit at room temperature for at least 30 minutes before grilling.

2 • Prepare a charcoal fire or preheat a gas grill for indirect grilling over medium heat (see pages 11–14).

3 • Remove the pork from the pan and discard the marinade. Grill the pork, covered, for 40 to 50 minutes, turning once, until an instant-read thermometer inserted in the thickest part of the meat registers at least 160 degrees F. The outside will be browned but not charred, and the meat will show just a blush of pink when cut.

4 • Remove the pork from the grill and place it on a cutting board. Cover the meat with a piece of aluminum foil to keep it warm, and allow the meat to rest for 5 minutes before slicing. Cut into 1/4-inch-thick slices and serve.

Makes 6 servings

# Grilled Ham Steak with Drunken Peaches

Bourbon-soaked, grilled peaches make a nice change from traditional pineapple.

---

½ cup plus 1 tablespoon bourbon
1 tablespoon Dijon mustard
2 teaspoons light brown sugar
Salt

Freshly ground pepper
1 (3-pound) ham steak, at least
1½ inches thick
8 ripe peaches, halved and pitted

---

1 • In a shallow pan, mix together 1 tablespoon of the bourbon with the mustard, brown sugar, salt, and pepper. Put the ham in the pan, and turn to coat. Let sit at room temperature for 30 minutes.

2 • Place the peaches, cut side down, in a shallow pan and pour the remaining ½ cup bourbon over the fruit. Let the peaches sit in the bourbon for at least 30 minutes.

3 • Prepare a charcoal fire or preheat a gas grill for direct grilling over medium heat (see pages 11–14).

4 • Remove the ham from the pan and transfer to the grill. Grill the ham, turning once, until crispy on both sides, 15 to 20 minutes.

5 • Remove the ham from the grill and place it on a cutting board. Cover the ham with a piece of aluminum foil to keep it warm, and allow the ham to rest for 5 minutes before slicing.

6 • While the ham is resting, remove the peaches from the bourbon and place them cut side down on the grill. Grill until the peaches begin to brown, 5 to 8 minutes. Turn over and grill briefly on the skin side. Discard the bourbon.

7 • Cut the ham into 8 pieces and serve immediately with the peaches on top.

*Makes 8 servings*

# Kebabs Cooked Right

Here's another opportunity to make something healthy that also satisfies your craving for meat. "Honey, look . . . veggies. Pay no attention to the red meat on the skewer . . . I am the great and powerful Kebab!"

Meat and vegetables on skewers look so pretty together—so it's especially disappointing when the meat is underdone or the vegetables burned. The problem is that meat and vegetables cook at different rates and different temperatures. The solution? Grill the meat on one set of skewers over direct high heat, while grilling the vegetables on a separate set of skewers over medium heat. This is easy on a gas grill; just preheat part of the grill to high and the other part to medium. If using a charcoal grill, cook the meat in the center of the grill, where coals are piled higher, and grill the vegetables around the edges. If you vary the vegetables—colorful bell peppers, mushrooms, and squash, for example—you will still have a feast for the eyes. (If you want to include cherry tomatoes, however, skewer them separately, as they cook much quicker than the other vegetables.) Separating the meat from the vegetables will also make your vegetarian guests happy.

## FOR THE MEAT

2 pounds lamb, beef, pork, or chicken, cut into 2-inch chunks
Marinade of your choice (pages 166–173)

## FOR THE VEGETABLES

2 pounds assorted vegetables such as bell peppers (all colors), mushrooms, leeks, onions, zucchini, and summer squash, cut into 1½-inch pieces; and cherry tomatoes

⅓ cup extra-virgin olive oil
2 tablespoons freshly squeezed lemon juice (from 1 lemon)
Salt
Freshly ground pepper

1 • Place the meat in a shallow, non-reactive pan and pour the marinade over it. Cover the pan and refrigerate for at least 8 hours and up to 24 hours, turning once during this time.

2 • Prepare a charcoal fire or preheat a gas grill for direct grilling, so that you have a medium heat and a high-heat area (see pages 11–14). If using bamboo skewers, soak them in water for at least 15 minutes to prevent them from burning.

3 • Remove the meat from the pan, discard the marinade, and thread the meat onto skewers. Make sure to leave a bit of space between the pieces, so that each piece cooks through.

4 • In a bowl, toss the vegetables with the oil, lemon juice, salt, and pepper. Thread them onto skewers. You can mix them up, except for the tomatoes, which should be skewered separately.

5 • Grill the meat over high heat for 12 to 15 minutes, turning the kebabs as they cook. Remove a chunk of meat from a skewer and slice it in half to see if it is cooked; beef and lamb can be pink inside, pork can be slightly pink, and chicken should be white throughout.

6 • While the meat is cooking, grill the vegetables over medium heat, turning, for 8 to 10 minutes or 4 minutes for cherry tomatoes. Serve immediately.

*Makes 6 servings*

# Satay

Satay-what? See, you have to say that like you're a "brutha" . . . Say what? Okay, it sounds funnier than it reads, but try it at your next barbecue after everyone's had a brew or two, and I guarantee screams!

For vegetarians, make this with seitan, a beef-like product made primarily of wheat gluten and available at health food stores and some supermarkets. If you are in a hurry, you can buy peanut dipping sauce in the supermarket for serving.

---

½ cup canned, unsweetened coconut
   milk
3 tablespoons whole milk
3 cloves garlic, peeled
3 (¼-inch-thick) slices peeled
   fresh ginger
1 tablespoon curry powder
1½ teaspoons ground coriander

1 teaspoon soy sauce
1 teaspoon salt
2 pounds boneless chicken, pork, or beef
   (or seitan) in any combination, cut
   into 1½-inch chunks or 1- by
   3-inch strips
Peanut Dipping Sauce (page 180)

---

1 • In the work bowl of a food processor or in a blender, mix together the coconut milk, whole milk, garlic, ginger, curry powder, coriander, soy sauce, and salt. Process until fairly smooth.

2 • Place the meat in a shallow, non-reactive pan and pour the marinade over it. Cover and refrigerate for at least 2 hours or up to 12, turning once during this time.

3 • Prepare a charcoal fire or preheat a gas grill for direct grilling over high heat (see pages 11–14). If using bamboo skewers, soak them in water for at least 15 minutes to prevent them from burning.

4 • Remove the meat from the pan, discard the marinade, and thread the meat onto skewers. Make sure to leave a bit of space between the pieces so that each piece cooks through.

5 • Grill the meat for 12 to 15 minutes, turning the skewers so that all sides get cooked.

Remove a chunk of meat from a skewer and slice it in half to see if it is cooked; beef and lamb can be pink inside, pork can be slightly pink, and chicken should be white throughout.

6 • Serve immediately with peanut dipping sauce, and Cucumber and Red Onion Salad (page 117), if desired.

*Makes 6 servings*

# Sheboygan Bratwurst

In Sheboygan, Wisconsin, a city that calls itself "The Bratwurst Capital of the World" (or "The Wurst City in the World"), folks will argue fiercely over the "right" way to grill a brat, the "correct" condiments, and the choice of beer to wash it all down with. Many Sheboyganites grill the bratwurst first, then simmer them briefly in beer, but I like the crispiness of the sausages when you do it the other way around. This method also works with other types of sausages. And let's face it, it's fun to say, "Sheboygan!" So, when you make this recipe, just before everyone digs in, have everyone yell: SHEBOYGAN!!!

12 bratwurst (3 pounds)
3 (12-ounce) cans beer
1¹/₂ cups water
2 large onions, peeled and thinly sliced

1 teaspoon freshly ground pepper
6 hard rolls
Coarse-grain mustard, ketchup, pickles, relish, sauerkraut, or other toppings

1 • Prick each bratwurst in several places with the tines of a fork. Put them in a large saucepan, and add the beer, water, onions, and pepper. Cover, bring to a boil over medium heat, then reduce the heat and simmer for 30 minutes.

2 • Prepare a charcoal fire or preheat a gas grill for direct grilling over high heat (see pages 11–14).

3 • Using tongs, remove the bratwurst from the beer. Transfer the bratwurst to the grill and cook, turning, for about 8 minutes, until browned on all sides.

4 • Drain the beer from the pot and discard it, but reserve the onions.

5 • Serve the bratwurst, 2 to a roll (a "double brat") with the onions and, if you are a traditionalist, with coarse-grain mustard. Otherwise, go to town with the condiments of your choice.

*Makes 6 servings*

# Fish and Seafood 101

I cannot emphasize enough how much I love grilling fish and seafood. Grilled shrimp or salmon is the best. And sea bass is my new favorite. It's firm and meaty and tastes fantastic just off the grill.

Buy firm fish with a fresh, saltwater smell. Steaks or fillets should be at least $3/4$ inch thick. Fish with a meat-like texture—swordfish, tuna, salmon, mahi-mahi—are perfect for the grill. Catfish fillets, halibut, and hake are also great on the grill. My trick for thin fillets (less than $1/2$ inch thick) is to put them in a grill basket, or to cook them—without turning them over—on a piece of oiled aluminum foil on the grill. This method also works for very fragile fish, like scrod and sole, which tend to fall apart no matter what. Count on serving $1/3$ to $1/2$ pound of fish fillets or steaks, $1/2$ pound shrimp, or 1 pound of shellfish (in the shell) per person.

# Fish Fillets with Lemon-Parsley Sauce

**FOR THE SAUCE**

| | |
|---|---|
| 1/2 cup chopped parsley leaves | 2 tablespoons capers, drained |
| 1/3 cup extra-virgin olive oil | Salt |
| 1 1/2 teaspoons finely grated lemon zest (from 1 lemon) | Freshly ground pepper |
| 3 tablespoons freshly squeezed lemon juice (from 1 lemon) | |

Whisk together all of the ingredients in a small bowl. Cover and refrigerate until ready to use, at least 1 hour, and up to 8 hours, to let the flavors blend.

**FOR THE FISH**

| | |
|---|---|
| 2 pounds fish fillets such as cod, catfish, haddock, halibut, hake, or monkfish | 2 to 3 tablespoons extra-virgin olive oil |
| | Salt |
| | Freshly ground pepper |

1 • Prepare a charcoal fire or preheat a gas grill for direct grilling over high heat (see pages 11–14). If you do not have a grill basket, lay a piece of oiled, heavy-duty aluminum foil—slightly larger than the fish—on the grill, and poke several holes in it.

2 • Using a pastry brush, generously coat both sides of the fish with oil, then season with salt and pepper.

3 • Place the fish on the grill, either in the grill basket or on the foil. If the fish has a skin,

place it skin side down. If using a grill basket, turn the fish once during grilling; if using the foil, do not turn it. Grill until the fish flakes when poked with a fork but is still a bit opaque in the center. The grilling time will vary according to the thickness of the fillets, but it should not take longer than 12 minutes total.

4 • Transfer the fish to a platter and drizzle with some of the parsley sauce. Serve with additional sauce on the side. The fish is excellent with grilled asparagus (page 107).

*Makes 4 servings*

# Salmon with Maple-Ginger Glaze

³/₄ cup maple syrup
¹/₃ cup balsamic vinegar
3 tablespoons peeled, minced fresh
    ginger
4 cloves garlic, peeled and minced
¹/₂ to ³/₄ teaspoon hot red pepper flakes

Salt
1 (3-pound) side of salmon, skin on,
    boned
3 to 4 tablespoons extra-virgin
    olive oil

1 • Prepare a charcoal fire or preheat a gas grill for direct grilling over medium heat (see pages 11–14).

2 •  In a small bowl, mix together the maple syrup, balsamic vinegar, ginger, garlic, red pepper flakes, and salt.

3 • Using a pastry brush, generously coat both sides of the salmon with the olive oil.

4 • Place the salmon, flesh side down, directly on the grill. Grill until the salmon loosens its grip on the grill—7 to 8 minutes. Turn carefully, then spoon the topping over the cooked side of the fish. Grill for 4 to 5 minutes more, until the topping has become like a glaze, and the salmon flakes when poked with a fork but is still a bit opaque in the center.

5 • Remove from the grill and serve immediately.

*Makes 6 servings*

# Citrus-Topped Sea Bass

Friends, you serve this at your next outdoor party, and if you don't get kissed on the lips by at least half of your guests, I will give you a personal weather forecast. Citrus keeps the fish tasting fresh and the sea bass will stand up to whatever your fire dishes out.

*3 tablespoons finely grated orange zest*
*(from 3 oranges)*
*2 tablespoons finely grated lemon zest*
*(from 4 lemons)*
*1 tablespoon finely grated lime zest*
*(from 2 to 3 limes)*
*3 cloves garlic, peeled and minced*
*2 tablespoons chopped parsley leaves*

*1 tablespoon chopped thyme leaves*
*1 teaspoon coarse salt, such as kosher*
*salt*
*1/2 teaspoon freshly ground pepper*
*1 tablespoon freshly squeezed lemon*
*juice (from 1 lemon)*
*3 pounds sea bass fillets*
*3 to 4 tablespoons extra-virgin olive oil*

1 • Prepare a charcoal fire or preheat a gas grill for direct grilling over high heat (see pages 11–14).

2 • In a small bowl, mix together the orange, lemon, and lime zests with the garlic, parsley, thyme, salt, and pepper. Moisten with the lemon juice and stir to form a gritty paste.

3 • Lay a piece of oiled, heavy-duty aluminum foil—slightly larger than the fish—on the grill, and poke several holes in it.

4 • Using a pastry brush, generously coat both sides of the fish with olive oil.

5 • Place the fish, skin side down, directly on the foil. Spoon the topping over the fish. Grill without turning for 12 to 15 minutes, or until the fish flakes when poked with a fork but is still a bit opaque in the center.

6 • Remove the fish from the grill and serve immediately.

*Makes 6 servings*

# Tuna Provençale

Yeah, I know. It sounds fancy, but what are you gonna do? I have editors who like names like these. I think I did a pretty good job of keeping this stuff from sounding too frou-frou, but you gotta pick your battles.

Tuna tastes best cooked rare, so buy thick ($3/4$ to 1 inch), sushi-quality tuna steaks from a reputable fish store. If you can't find good tuna, or you like the fish cooked through, buy thinner ($1/2$-inch-thick) steaks.

1 cup extra-virgin olive oil
6 cloves garlic, peeled and minced
2 large shallots, peeled and finely chopped
8 medium tomatoes (2$1/2$ pounds), stemmed and roughly chopped
$1/2$ cup chopped basil leaves

$1/4$ cup drained capers
Salt
Freshly ground pepper
3 pounds sushi-quality tuna steaks (also called "ahi" or "yellowfin"), each $3/4$ to 1 inch thick

1 • Prepare a charcoal fire or preheat a gas grill for direct grilling over high heat (see pages 11–14).

2 • While the grill is heating, make the sauce. In a skillet, heat $3/4$ cup of the oil over medium heat. Add the garlic and shallots, and cook, stirring, for 3 to 5 minutes, until the shallots and garlic begin to soften but not to brown. Put the chopped tomatoes in a bowl, and pour the garlic, shallots, and oil over them. Add the basil, capers, salt, and pepper, and toss. Set aside.

3 • Using a pastry brush, generously coat both sides of each of the tuna steaks using the remaining $1/4$ cup oil, and season with salt and pepper. Grill for about 3 minutes per side for rare, or 6 minutes per side for medium.

4 • Serve immediately, topped with the tomato sauce. Serve with good French or Italian bread for mopping up extra sauce.

*Makes 6 servings*

# Shrimp with Cilantro-Mint Pesto

*4 pounds fresh or frozen large or extra-large shrimp (21 to 25 count per pound), in the shell*
*Cilantro-Mint Pesto (page 179)*

1 • If using frozen shrimp, thaw them according to the package directions. Whether using fresh or frozen (and thawed) shrimp, remove the shells. If you wish to devein the shrimp, cut along the vein with a sharp knife. Or, you can just skip the deveining process. The vein won't hurt you.

2 • Toss the shelled shrimp with the pesto in a shallow, non-reactive pan. Each shrimp should be well coated. Cover with plastic wrap and refrigerate for 1 to 2 hours.

3 • Prepare a charcoal fire or preheat a gas grill for direct grilling over high heat (see pages 11–14).

4 • Remove the shrimp from the pan and discard the marinade. Grill the shrimp for 2 to 3 minutes per side. To test for doneness, take a shrimp off the grill and cut the shrimp in half; the flesh should be white and firm throughout. Serve immediately.

*Makes 8 main-course servings, or 12 appetizer servings*

# New Orleans–Style Barbecued Shrimp

In New Orleans, BBQ shrimp is actually cooked in a pan on the stovetop. This is an adaptation for the grill. Cover the picnic table with brown paper, get a stack of paper napkins, and go to town. Don't blame me if that loudmouth Emeril Lagasse shows up. I'm kidding. Really. BAM!

4 pounds fresh or frozen large or extra-large shrimp (21 to 25 count per pound), in the shell
5 tablespoons chili powder
1 tablespoon plus 2 teaspoons salt
16 tablespoons (2 sticks) unsalted butter
2 medium onions, peeled and finely chopped
6 cloves garlic, peeled and minced
1 cup ketchup
1/2 cup extra-virgin olive oil

5 tablespoons light brown sugar
1/4 cup Worcestershire sauce
1 lemon, sliced
3 tablespoons freshly squeezed lemon juice (from 1 lemon)
3 bay leaves
2 teaspoons dried oregano
2 teaspoons dried thyme
1 teaspoon cayenne pepper
Several dashes Louisiana-style hot sauce

1 • You can buy large, frozen tiger shrimp that have been deveined but are still in the shell. If you use these, thaw them according to the package directions. If using fresh shrimp, you can ask the person at the fish counter to devein them for you in the shell. You can also do this yourself, using kitchen shears. Cut the shell along the vein and pull the vein out with your fingers. Or, you can just skip the deveining process. The vein won't hurt you.

2 • Combine 3 tablespoons of the chili powder and 1 tablespoon of the salt in a small bowl. Rub the shrimp with this mixture, making sure you rub some into the open cut where the shrimp has been deveined (if it has) to season the shrimp inside the shell. Place the shrimp in a shallow, non-reactive pan, cover with plastic wrap, and refrigerate while you make the sauce.

3 • In a saucepan set over medium-high heat, melt the butter. Add the onion and garlic and cook for 3 to 5 minutes, until soft but not browned. Add the ketchup, oil, brown sugar,

Worcestershire sauce, lemon slices, lemon juice, bay leaves, oregano, thyme, cayenne, and hot sauce, as well as the remaining 2 tablespoons chili powder and 2 teaspoons salt. Stir to mix. Reduce the heat to a simmer, and cook, covered, stirring occasionally, for about 20 minutes, or until thick. Remove from the heat, uncover, and cool to room temperature. Remove and discard the lemon slices and bay leaves.

4 • Pour 1 1/2 cups of the sauce over the shrimp. Toss to coat well. Cover and refrigerate the shrimp for 1 to 2 hours. Cover and refrigerate the remaining sauce separately and save for dipping.

5 • Prepare a charcoal fire or preheat a gas grill for direct grilling over high heat (see pages 11–14).

6 • While the grill is heating, reheat the remaining sauce in a small, covered saucepan over very low heat—it will only take a few minutes. Watch the sauce carefully so that it doesn't burn.

7 • Remove the shrimp from the pan and discard the marinade. Grill the shrimp for 2 to 3 minutes per side, until the shells are orangy-pink. To test for doneness, take a shrimp off the grill, remove the shell, and cut the shrimp in half: The flesh should be white and firm throughout.

8 • Serve with the warm sauce for dipping, and a large bowl for the shells.

*Makes 8 main-course servings, or 12 appetizer servings*

# Grill-Steamed Mussels and Clams

Remember when you were in the Scouts and you made "hobo packets"? Well, this is a seafood version of that.

---

2 pounds mussels (about 48), bearded
    (see Note) and well rinsed under
    cold running water
2½ pounds littleneck clams (about 24),
    well rinsed under cold running
    water
8 tablespoons (1 stick) unsalted butter

¼ cup chopped parsley leaves
4 cloves garlic, peeled and minced
1 teaspoon hot red pepper flakes
½ cup white wine
¼ cup freshly squeezed lemon juice
    (from 1 to 2 lemons)

---

1 • Discard any mussels or clams with broken shells, as well as those whose shells remain open after you tap them lightly.

2 • Prepare a charcoal fire or preheat a gas grill for direct grilling over high heat (see pages 11–14).

3 • Cut 4 sheets of heavy-duty aluminum foil, each 18 by 24 inches. Set them flat on a work surface.

4 • In the center of each sheet of foil, pile one-quarter of the mussels (about a dozen) and one-quarter of the clams (about a half dozen). Cut the butter into small pieces and dot each mound of shellfish with about 2 tablespoons of butter. Sprinkle each mound with one-quarter of the parsley, garlic, and red pepper flakes. Pour 2 tablespoons of wine and 1 tablespoon of lemon juice over each pile of shellfish.

5 • Bring up the 2 long sides of the packets and fold them over each other 2 or 3 times at the edge where they meet to seal, leaving some room inside for the mussels and clams to expand as they cook. Fold the shorter ends of the foil over themselves 2 or 3 times as well. The packet should be well sealed.

6 • Carefully transfer the packets, seam side up, onto the grill and cook until the shellfish open, 8 to 10 minutes. (You'll have to peek into one packet to make sure.)

7 • Serve the mussels and clams in the foil packets with crusty bread for mopping up the sauce, or, if you want to be more elegant, put the shellfish in a bowl, pouring the packet juices on top. You can also serve the mussels, clams, and their juices directly over cooked linguine. Make sure to discard any of the shellfish that do not open after cooking.

**NOTE:** "Bearding" mussels means removing the tough, weedy string that is often attached to them. Use a dish cloth or towel to get a good grip on the beard and pull it off.

*Makes 4 servings*

# Side Shows

# Tropical Fruit Salsa

I am a big fan of salsa, all kinds of salsa. It's a great way to get your kids to eat their veggies and think they're having a good time. This salsa complements all sorts of dishes, but especially chicken, pork, or fish.

*2 mangos*
*2 kiwis, peeled*
*1/2 medium red onion, peeled and finely*
*    chopped*
*1/2 medium red bell pepper, stemmed,*
*    seeded, and chopped*
*3 tablespoons freshly squeezed lime*
*    juice (from 1 to 2 limes)*

*2 tablespoons chopped cilantro leaves*
*2 tablespoons chopped mint leaves*
*1/2 teaspoon hot red pepper flakes*
*Salt*
*Freshly ground pepper*

1 • Peel the mango by making 4 lengthwise incisions in the skin with a sharp knife, then pulling off the skin. Working on a cutting board with a sharp knife, slice the flesh away from the pit. Chop the flesh and place it in a serving bowl.

2 • Slice the kiwis into 1/4-inch-thick rounds and then cut the rounds in half. Mix the kiwi with the mango. Stir in all of the remaining ingredients.

3 • Cover and refrigerate for up to 1 hour before serving. Leftovers, unfortunately, do not keep well, but you probably won't have any.

*Makes about 4 cups, or 8 servings*

# Best Baked Beans

If you are really serious about having a successful barbecue, you have got to have baked beans. Yeah, I know, you're expecting some sort of flatulence joke here, right? Well, I'm not going to stoop that low. Well, maybe I'll stoop a little.

Guy in Manhattan goes to his doctor and says, "Doc, you gotta help me. I have been having the worst gas!" Doctor says, "Okay, Mr. Jones. I want you to take one of these pills each day for the next week. The symptoms will actually increase, but then you'll be cured. If there are any problems, call me."

The poor guy starts the regimen, but after the fifth day, the force and frequency are unbearable. Finally he breaks down and calls his doctor back. "Doc, it's really bad. I can't move. Can you come help me?" "All right, I'll be right there," his doctor answers. "Where are you?" The guy replies, "Okay, you remember where Macy's used to be . . . ?"

1 pound dried Navy beans, picked over
   and rinsed
4 slices thick-cut bacon, or 6 slices
   regular bacon
1 medium onion, peeled and finely
   chopped

$1/2$ cup packed dark brown sugar
$1/4$ cup dark molasses
$1/4$ cup ketchup
1 tablespoon spicy brown mustard
1 teaspoon salt
$1^1/2$ to $2^1/2$ cups apple cider or water

1 • Put the beans in a large pot and add enough cold water to cover them by 2 inches. Soak the beans overnight in a cool place.

2 • Drain the beans and return them to the pot. Add enough cold water to cover by 2 inches. Cover the pot, set it over high heat, and bring the water to a boil. Reduce the heat to a simmer and cook the beans, covered, until tender, 45 minutes to 1 hour. Remove the pot from the heat and drain the beans in a colander. Dry the pot.

3 • Preheat the oven to 250 degrees F.

4 • Put the bacon in the pot, and put the pot over medium-high heat. Cook the bacon for a couple of minutes or so until it releases about 1 tablespoon of fat. Remove the bacon

from the pot using a slotted spoon—reserve the bacon fat in the pot—and chop half of the slices. Set the chopped bacon and whole strips aside for the moment.

5 • Add the onion to the pot with the bacon fat, and sauté over medium heat for 5 minutes, or until the onion is soft but not browned. Return the beans to the pot, and add the chopped bacon, brown sugar, molasses, ketchup, mustard, and salt. Stir well. Top with the remaining whole strips of bacon.

6 • Pour in enough cider or water so you can just see it seeping through the top of the beans. Bake, covered, for 2 hours. Remove the cover and bake an additional 3 to 4 hours, or until the beans are dark and very tender. If the beans seem to be drying out, add more cider or water as needed.

7 • Serve the beans hot, from the pot.

*Makes 6 servings*

*To doctor store-bought canned baked beans, try adding some finely chopped onion, a few tablespoons of ketchup or BBQ sauce (pages 184–187), some spicy brown or Dijon mustard, and a bit of dark molasses or maple syrup. On the other hand, you may wanna try making your own.*

# My Mom's Peas and Rice

In the Caribbean and in the South, some beans are known as "peas." For example, black-eyed peas, which are really beans. You could call this recipe beans and rice, but then maybe you'd get confused with franks and beans. All I know is, it tastes great.

My mother has made her patented peas and rice for family picnics and barbecues since I was a little boy. I think that was her way of making sure she would get invited. She is known far and wide for her peas and rice, and with good reason. Her only nod to convenience is to use canned kidney beans.

---

*½ pound salt pork, cut into 4 chunks*
*1 medium onion, peeled and finely*
*    chopped*
*6 cloves garlic, peeled and minced*
*1 green bell pepper, stemmed, seeded,*
*    and finely chopped*

*3 cups white rice*
*6 cups water*
*Salt*
*Freshly ground pepper*
*3 (15-ounce) cans red kidney beans,*
*    drained, rinsed, and drained again*

---

1 • Place a large pot over medium-high heat, and add the salt pork. Cook for several minutes, until the pork renders a tablespoon or so of fat. Add the onion, garlic, and bell pepper to the pot, lower the heat to medium-low, and continue to cook, stirring, until the onions are translucent, 5 to 7 minutes.

2 • Add the rice to the pot and stir to combine. Pour in the water and season with salt and pepper. Bring to a boil over high heat, then reduce the heat to a simmer and cook, covered, for 20 minutes.

3 • Stir the beans into the rice and cook for 10 minutes more. Remove the salt pork and discard. Serve immediately.

*Makes 8 servings*

# Wild Rice Salad with Toasted Almonds

3/4 cup wild rice
1/2 cup white rice
1/3 cup extra-virgin olive oil
1/4 cup red wine vinegar
1 cup golden raisins
3/4 cup chopped almonds, toasted
    (see below)

1/2 cup pitted black olives
1/4 cup chopped parsley leaves
1 jalapeño pepper, stemmed, seeded,
    and finely chopped
Salt
Freshly ground pepper
1 cup cherry or grape tomatoes, halved

1 • Rinse the wild rice well. Cook according to the package directions, omitting any salt or butter that is called for.

2 • In a separate saucepan, cook the white rice according to the package directions, omitting any salt or butter that is called for.

3 • When both types of rice are cooked, combine them in a large serving bowl. Add the oil and vinegar, and mix well. At this point you can cover the bowl with plastic wrap and refrigerate for several hours or overnight. Bring to room temperature before proceeding.

4 • Just before serving, mix the raisins, almonds, olives, parsley, and jalapeño pepper into the rice. Season with salt and pepper to taste. Gently stir in the tomatoes. Serve immediately.

*Makes 6 servings*

## To Toast Nuts

*Preheat the oven to 325 degrees F. Put the nuts in an ovenproof skillet and toast them in the oven until fragrant, 5 to 10 minutes. Watch them carefully, so that they don't burn. Remove the skillet from the oven, remove the nuts from the skillet (or they will continue to cook), and set them aside to cool.*

# Corn, Black Bean, and Tomato Salad

We have a house in Columbia County, New York, and one of the great simple pleasures of the summer is when the fresh corn comes in at a local stand called Brosen's. The corn is so sweet, you can actually eat it raw, like an apple.

I love grilling corn. The direct heat caramelizes the sugar in the corn, making it even sweeter, while giving it a crunch and a nuttiness that boiling in water could never impart.

Whenever I'm grilling corn, I always throw a couple of extra ears on the grill so that I can make this salad later on during the weekend. It's always a hit and the textures of the grilled corn, the beans, and the tomatoes really go well together.

## FOR THE DRESSING

3 tablespoons freshly squeezed lime
    juice (from 1 to 2 limes)
3 tablespoons rice vinegar
3 tablespoons peanut oil

½ teaspoon sugar
¼ teaspoon hot red pepper flakes
Salt

In a small bowl, whisk together all of the ingredients. Cover and refrigerate until needed, or for up to 2 days.

## FOR THE SALAD

2 ears corn, husked
1 (19-ounce) can black beans, drained,
    rinsed, and drained again
2 medium tomatoes (¾ pound), cored
    and chopped

1 large shallot, peeled and finely
    chopped
¼ cup chopped cilantro leaves

1 • Prepare a charcoal fire or preheat a gas grill for direct cooking over high heat (see pages 11–14).

2 • Grill the corn for 8 to 12 minutes, until the kernels look toasty and a few are dark brown. When cool enough to handle, cut a small slice off the fattest end of the corn. Stand the ear on the flat end in a medium bowl and, using a sharp knife, cut the corn off the cob. You should have about 2 cups of kernels.

3 • Add the black beans, tomatoes, shallot, and cilantro to the bowl, and mix gently. Drizzle with the dressing, and mix again. Let sit at room temperature for at least 30 minutes or up to 2 hours, for the flavors to blend before serving.

*Makes 6 servings*

# Deborah's Perry, Georgia, Potato Salad

This is a "classic" potato salad that my wife, Deborah, makes frequently. It is the kind of potato salad made by folks in her hometown of Perry, Georgia. In the South, I think it's a criminal offense for there to be a barbecue without potato salad or cole slaw.

If you are buying potato salad at a deli or grocery store, consider these possible additions to jazz it up: crumbled bacon, chopped parsley, capers, chopped dill pickles, chopped green apples (such as Granny Smiths), sliced celery, Worcestershire sauce, hot sauce, fresh or dried dill, caraway seeds, or Italian dressing.

6 medium white or Yukon Gold
   potatoes (3 pounds)
3 large eggs
1/2 Vidalia onion, peeled and finely
   chopped
1/4 cup chopped pimento

3 tablespoons sweet pickle relish
1/2 cup mayonnaise
1/2 cup spicy brown mustard
Salt
Freshly ground pepper
1/2 teaspoon paprika

1 • Peel the potatoes and cut them into 1 1/2-inch chunks. Put them in a pot and add water to cover by about 2 inches. Salt the water generously. Cover the pot and set it over high heat. Bring the water to a boil, then add the eggs. Reduce the heat to a brisk simmer and cook, covered, until the potatoes can just be pierced by a fork, about 15 minutes.

2 • With a slotted spoon, remove the eggs from the pot and set them aside. Drain the potatoes and place them in a large bowl. Rinse the eggs under cold running water until cool enough to handle. Peel and chop 2 of the eggs and add them to the potatoes. Add the onion, pimento, and relish to the potatoes.

3 • In a small bowl, mix together the mayonnaise and mustard. Spoon over the potato salad, season with salt and pepper, and mix gently.

4 • Peel the remaining egg and slice it, placing the slices on top of the potato salad. Sprinkle with the paprika.

5 • Serve immediately or cover with plastic wrap and refrigerate for up to 4 hours. Serve chilled or at room temperature.

*Makes 6 servings*

# Grilled Potato Salad with Crisp Bacon

*1/2 cup mayonnaise*

*2 tablespoons cider vinegar*

*2 tablespoons canola oil, or other*
   *vegetable oil*

*Salt*

*Freshly ground pepper*

In a small bowl, whisk together all of the ingredients. Cover and refrigerate until needed, or for up to 2 days.

**FOR THE SALAD**

*4 pounds small (3-inch) red potatoes*

*6 tablespoons extra-virgin olive oil*

*Coarse salt, such as kosher salt*

*Freshly ground pepper*

*6 strips bacon*

*1 medium red onion, peeled and thinly*
   *sliced*

*1/2 cup chopped parsley leaves*

1 • Scrub the potatoes, put them in a large pot, and add water to cover by about 2 inches. Salt the water generously. Cover the pot and set it over high heat. Bring the water to a boil, then reduce the heat to a brisk simmer and cook until the potatoes can just be pierced by a fork. The time will vary with the size of your potatoes, but they may take up to 25 minutes.

2 • Drain the potatoes, place them in a shallow pan, and drizzle with the oil. Roll the potatoes in the oil to coat, season with salt and pepper, and let cool to room temperature. Cut the potatoes in half, and toss to coat the cut sides in oil. You can do this several hours ahead of time; let the potatoes sit at room temperature.

3 • Prepare a charcoal fire or preheat a gas grill for direct cooking over high heat (see pages 11–14).

4 • While the grill is heating, warm a skillet over medium-high heat. Add the bacon and cook, turning as needed, until crisp, 12 to 15 minutes. Remove the bacon from the skillet and drain on paper towels. When it's cool, chop roughly and set aside.

5 • Grill the potatoes, turning them frequently, until they are well browned and beginning to char in spots, 5 to 8 minutes. Put them in a bowl, and add the bacon, onion, and parsley.

6 • Drizzle the dressing over the potatoes, toss gently, and serve immediately.

*Makes 8 servings*

# Pasta Salad with Parmesan and Basil

I know there are those who look down their collective noses at pasta salad, but I think if it's done right it's a great addition to any gathering. Try this one if the Sopranos are coming over. Try not coming back for seconds . . . "Just when I thought I was out . . . they pull me back in!"

It is easier to grate zest from a whole lemon than one that has been squeezed. Before you squeeze the lemon for the dressing, grate the zest for the salad.

**FOR THE DRESSING**

| | |
|---|---|
| ¼ cup freshly squeezed lemon juice (from 1 to 2 lemons) | 1 cup extra-virgin olive oil |
| | Coarse salt, such as kosher salt |
| 2 tablespoons Dijon mustard | Freshly ground pepper |

In a small bowl, whisk together the lemon juice and mustard. Slowly drizzle in the oil, whisking to emulsify. Season with salt and pepper. Cover and refrigerate until needed, or for up to 2 days.

**FOR THE SALAD**

| | |
|---|---|
| 1 pound bow-tie pasta, shells, or other medium-sized, shaped pasta | 3 tablespoons chopped parsley leaves |
| 1 cup frozen petite peas, thawed | 1 tablespoon finely grated lemon zest (from 2 lemons) |
| ½ cup freshly grated Parmesan cheese | 2 cloves garlic, peeled and minced |
| ½ cup imported black olives, such as Kalamata, pitted and sliced in half | 1 teaspoon hot red pepper flakes, optional |
| | ¼ cup chopped basil leaves |

1 • Bring a large pot of salted water to a boil, add the pasta, and cook according to the package directions until "al dente" (cooked, but still firm). Drain well. Put the pasta in a large bowl and drizzle with $^3/_4$ cup of the dressing. Cover and refrigerate the remaining dressing; you should have slightly more than $^1/_2$ cup left.

2 • Add the peas, $^1/_4$ cup of the cheese, the olives, parsley, lemon zest, garlic, and red pepper flakes (if using) to the pasta. Toss to coat. Cover with plastic wrap and refrigerate until chilled, at least 2 hours and up to 8.

3 • Just before serving, add the remaining dressing, the remaining $^1/_4$ cup Parmesan cheese, and the basil. Toss gently and serve.

*Makes 8 servings*

# Grilled Bread Salad

It's like having a great sandwich, only it's a salad. Is this a great country or what?

6 medium ripe tomatoes (2 pounds),
stemmed and chopped
1 medium red onion, peeled and thinly
sliced
3 tablespoons balsamic vinegar
Coarse salt, such as kosher salt

Freshly ground pepper
3/4 cup extra-virgin olive oil
2 cloves garlic, peeled and halved
1 (1-pound) loaf day-old crusty bread,
cut into 1-inch slices
1/2 cup chopped basil leaves

1 • Prepare a charcoal fire or preheat a gas grill for direct cooking over high heat (see pages 11–14).

2 • While the grill is heating, combine the tomatoes, onion, vinegar, salt, and pepper in a large bowl. Drizzle with 1/4 cup of the oil.

3 • Using a pastry brush, coat both sides of each slice of bread with oil, using about 1/4 cup total. Grill the bread for 1 to 2 minutes on each side, until well toasted. Rub both sides of each toasted slice with the cut side of a garlic clove. Cut each slice of bread into bite-sized cubes. Discard the garlic. Toss the bread cubes with the tomato mixture and the basil and drizzle with the remaining 1/4 cup oil. Serve immediately.

*Makes 6 servings*

## Grilled Vegetables 101

Here's a tip of the hat to those who want us to eat healthy. I gotta admit that I really love grilled veggies. The snap of grilled asparagus, the meatiness of mushrooms, and the sweetness of onions and peppers are a nice way to eat well and enjoy it too. I always include some grilled veggies for those vegans in the bunch, if they're not already in a semi-state of meat catatonia.

The basic method for grilling vegetables is to coat them with extra-virgin olive oil ($\frac{1}{3}$ to $\frac{1}{2}$ cup will suffice for 2 pounds of veggies), and season them with salt and freshly ground pepper. Most vegetables should be grilled over direct medium heat; grill corn over direct high heat (see pages 11–14).

### Asparagus

Cut or snap off the tough ends before cooking. Lay the spears in a shallow bowl, drizzle them with extra-virgin olive oil, and season with salt and freshly ground pepper, turning to coat. Grill over direct medium heat for 6 to 8 minutes, turning, until nicely browned. Drizzle with more olive oil and sprinkle with freshly grated Parmesan cheese, if desired, before serving.

### Corn

There are two main ways to grill corn: unhusked and husked. Cooking corn in the husk requires removing the corn silk (without actually husking the corn), soaking the corn in water, and grilling it for well over 30 minutes. It's a production, and in my opinion does not give the corn that great grilled flavor I'm looking for. I prefer a simpler method: Husk the corn and grill it for 8 to 12 minutes over direct high heat, turning as you grill. If you want, you can coat each ear with melted butter (about 1 tablespoon per ear) before grilling; this creates a few flare-ups that will give the corn a nice sizzled taste. Serve with additional butter and salt.

### Eggplant, Baby

Stem and cut each eggplant lengthwise in half. Using a pastry brush, generously coat both sides with extra-virgin olive oil, and season with salt and freshly ground pepper. Grill over direct medium heat, turning once, for 10 to 15 minutes, until tender.

### Eggplant, Globe

Stem and cut the eggplant into 3/4-inch-thick rounds. Salt the rounds heavily on both sides, place them on several layers of paper towels, cover them with more paper towels, and place several weights on top (cookbooks work well). Let sit for 30 minutes to remove the bitterness in the eggplant. Rinse the eggplant slices thoroughly and pat dry. Using a pastry brush, generously coat both sides of each round with extra-virgin olive oil, and season with freshly ground pepper. Grill, turning once, over direct medium heat, for 12 to 15 minutes, until tender. Splash with balsamic vinegar, if desired, just before serving.

### Fennel

Cut off the leafy tops and trim the root end from the fennel. Slice each bulb in half length-wise. Using a pastry brush, generously coat both sides of each bulb with extra-virgin olive oil, and season with salt and freshly ground pepper. Grill for about 20 minutes over direct medium heat, turning halfway through, until tender.

### Mushrooms, Domestic

Stem and clean the mushrooms by wiping them with a damp paper towel. Place them in a shallow bowl, drizzle them with extra-virgin olive oil, and season them with salt and freshly ground pepper, tossing to coat. Thread the mushrooms onto skewers. (If using bamboo skewers, soak them in water for at least 15 minutes before threading to prevent them from burning.) Grill the mushrooms over direct medium heat for 7 to 10 minutes, turning once, and basting with additional oil, as needed, until tender.

### Mushrooms, Portobello

Stem the mushrooms. You can leave the dark gills on the underside; they give the mushrooms a more intense flavor. If you choose to remove the gills, use the edge of a teaspoon to scoop them out. Wipe the mushrooms clean with a damp paper towel. Using a pastry brush, generously coat both sides of each mushroom with extra-virgin olive oil, and season with salt and freshly ground pepper. Grill over direct medium heat for 12 to 15 minutes, turning once, and basting with additional oil, as needed, until tender.

## Onions, Spanish, Vidalia, Red, or Other

Peel the onions and slice them crosswise into $1/2$-inch-thick slices. Carefully thread each whole slice onto a skewer. (If using bamboo skewers, soak them in water for at least 15 minutes before threading to prevent them from burning.) Thread only one slice of onion onto each skewer, making sure the skewer passes through each ring of the onion; when done, the skewer and onion will resemble a lollipop. Using a pastry brush, generously coat both sides of each onion slice with extra-virgin olive oil, and season with salt and freshly ground pepper. Grill over direct medium heat, turning once, for 10 to 15 minutes, until tender. Remove the onions from the skewers, place the onions in a bowl, and splash them with balsamic vinegar, if desired, before serving.

## Peppers, Bell

Stem, seed, and cut the peppers into large chunks. Place them in a shallow bowl, drizzle them with extra-virgin olive oil, and season with salt and freshly ground pepper, turning to coat. Put the peppers on the grill as is, or thread onto skewers. (If using bamboo skewers, soak them in water for at least 15 minutes before threading to prevent them from burning.) Cook the peppers over direct medium heat for 8 to 10 minutes, turning them as needed, until the edges begin to char. Splash with balsamic vinegar, if desired, before serving. (If you want very tender, peeled, roasted bell peppers, follow the directions on page 40.)

## Squash, Zucchini and Summer

Cut the squash on the diagonal into long, $1/2$-inch-thick pieces. Using a pastry brush, generously coat both sides of each slice with extra-virgin olive oil, and season with salt and freshly ground pepper. Grill over direct medium heat, turning once, for 10 to 15 minutes,

Jerk Chicken (page 60) with Tropical Fruit Salsa (page 93)

*Grill-Steamed Mussels and Clams (page 88) over pasta*

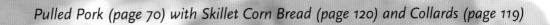
*Pulled Pork (page 70) with Skillet Corn Bread (page 120) and Collards (page 119)*

Grilled Potato Salad with Crisp Bacon (page 102)

*Marinated Pork Tenderloin (page 72)*

Turkey on the Grill (page 61) with
Wild Rice Salad with Toasted Almonds (page 97)

*Grilled corn and vegetables (page 107)*

*New Orleans–Style Barbecued Shrimp (page 86)*

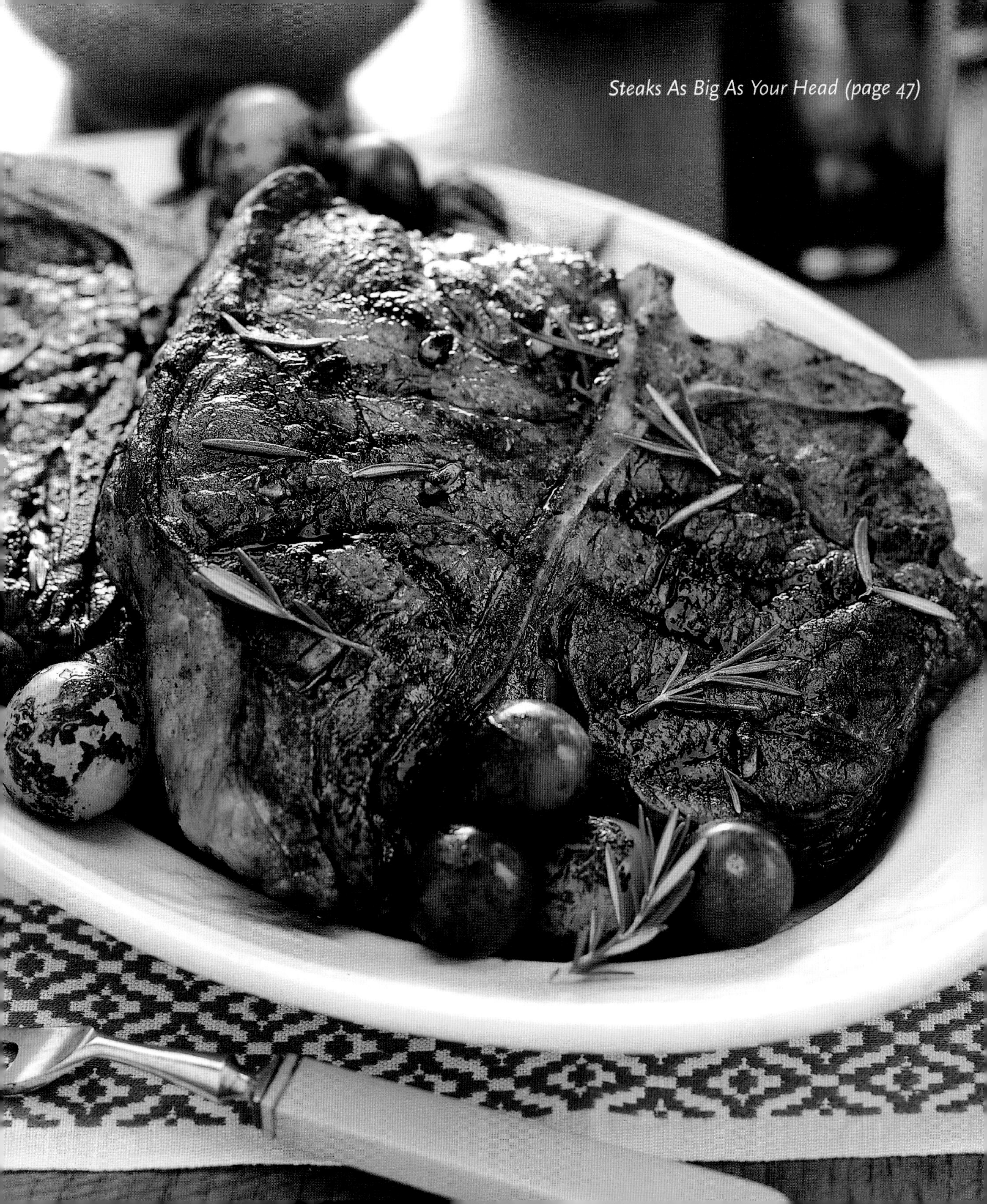

*Steaks As Big As Your Head (page 47)*

*Kebabs Cooked Right (page 74)*
*with Iced Tea (page 160)*

Chicken Caesar Salad with Grilled Croutons (page 56)

*Rustic Blackberry Tart (page 140)*

*Perfect Peach Ice Cream (page 150)*
*with Raspberry Sauce (page 154)*

*Frozen Watermelon Daiquiris (page 162)*

Blueberry Cobbler (page 134)

Peach Pie (page 136)

until tender. Splash the squash with additional oil and some freshly squeezed lemon juice, if desired, before serving.

## Tomatoes, Cherry

Stem the tomatoes and thread them onto skewers. (If using bamboo skewers, soak them in water for at least 15 minutes before threading to prevent them from burning.) Grill over direct medium heat for about 4 minutes, turning occasionally, until the tomatoes are soft and begin to char. Season with salt and freshly ground pepper before serving.

# Classic Cole Slaw

Cole slaw is a must for barbecue, especially if you're having Pulled Pork (page 70) or ribs (pages 66–69). It evokes memories of picnics from long ago. Don't go with the glop they serve at your deli. Odds are it's some commercial concoction that has no crunch or bite. If there's a side dish you want to take the time to make from scratch, it's slaw.

## FOR THE DRESSING

| | |
|---|---|
| ½ cup mayonnaise | 2 teaspoons sugar, or more, to taste |
| ¼ cup canola oil, or other vegetable oil | 1 teaspoon Dijon mustard |
| 2 tablespoons cider vinegar | |

In a small bowl, whisk together all of the ingredients. Cover and refrigerate for at least 30 minutes and up to 2 days, for the flavors to blend.

## FOR THE SLAW

| | |
|---|---|
| ¼ large green cabbage | ½ green bell pepper, stemmed, seeded, and thinly sliced |
| ¼ medium red cabbage | |
| 2 carrots, peeled | ½ red bell pepper, stemmed, seeded, and thinly sliced |
| ½ large Vidalia onion, peeled and thinly sliced | ½ cup chopped parsley leaves |

1 • Using a sharp knife, core the cabbages. Finely shred the cabbages with a sharp knife, or in the work bowl of a food processor fitted with a slicing blade. You should have about 5 cups of green cabbage and 4 cups of red cabbage. Shred the carrots in the food processor, or on the largest holes of a box grater.

2 • In a large bowl, mix together the cabbage, carrots, onion, and bell peppers. You can do this several hours ahead of time. Cover the bowl with plastic wrap and refrigerate.

3 • At least 30 minutes before serving, pour the dressing over the cole slaw, add the parsley, and toss. Serve at room temperature, or chilled, within 1 hour of adding the dressing.

*Makes 8 servings*

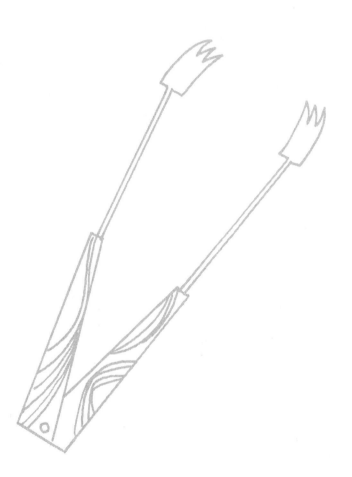

# Asian Slaw

Some folks prefer a vinegar-based cole slaw, instead of one that is mayonnaise-based. This recipe adds a little twist to the vinegar-based slaw and has a little bite to it, thanks to the red pepper flakes. You can add more or less, depending on your desire for heat.

## FOR THE DRESSING

1/3 cup rice vinegar

3 tablespoons peanut oil

2 tablespoons sugar

1 tablespoon Asian sesame oil

1 tablespoon peeled, minced
    fresh ginger

2 cloves garlic, peeled and minced

2 tablespoons freshly squeezed lime
    juice (from 1 lime)

2 teaspoons salt

1 teaspoon hot red pepper flakes

In a small bowl, whisk together all of the ingredients. Cover and refrigerate for at least 30 minutes and up to 2 days, for the flavors to blend.

## FOR THE SALAD

1/4 large green cabbage

1/4 medium red cabbage

2 carrots, peeled

1 large Granny Smith apple, stemmed,
    cored, and chopped

6 scallions, white and green parts
    chopped

1/2 cup chopped cilantro leaves

1 • Using a sharp knife, core the cabbages. Finely shred them with a sharp knife, or in the work bowl of a food processor fitted with a slicing blade. You should have about 5 cups of green cabbage and 4 cups of red cabbage. Shred the carrots in the food processor, or on the largest holes of a box grater.

2 • In a large bowl, mix together the cabbage, carrots, apples, and scallions. You can do this several hours ahead of time. Cover the bowl with plastic wrap and refrigerate.

3 • At least 30 minutes before serving, pour the dressing over the cole slaw, add the cilantro, and toss. Serve at room temperature within 1 hour of adding the dressing.

*Makes 8 servings*

# Summertime Green Bean Salad

2 pounds green beans, trimmed
5 cloves garlic, peeled
2/3 cup extra-virgin olive oil
1/4 cup balsamic vinegar
1 pint cherry or grape tomatoes, halved

1/2 large Vidalia onion, peeled and
    finely chopped
1 cup imported olives, preferably
    Niçoise, pitted
1/2 cup freshly grated Parmesan cheese

1 • Fill a large pot with salted water, set it over high heat, and bring the water to a boil. Add the beans and 2 cloves of garlic. Cook until the beans are tender but still have some snap to them, 8 to 12 minutes. Drain the beans and immediately run them under cold running water to stop the cooking. When cool, drain again. Discard the garlic. Put the beans in a bowl and immediately douse with the oil and vinegar.

2 • Finely chop the remaining 3 cloves of garlic. Add them to the beans along with the remaining ingredients, and toss. Serve immediately or cover with plastic wrap and refrigerate for up to 4 hours. Serve chilled or at room temperature.

*Makes 8 servings*

# Cucumber and Red Onion Salad

**FOR THE DRESSING**

¼ cup cider vinegar
2 tablespoons sugar
1 tablespoon canola oil, or other
    vegetable oil

¼ teaspoon hot red pepper flakes

In a small bowl, whisk together all of the ingredients. Cover and refrigerate until needed, or for up to 2 days.

**FOR THE SALAD**

3 large cucumbers, halved lengthwise
    and thinly sliced (see Note)
Coarse salt, such as kosher salt
Freshly ground pepper

1 large red onion, peeled and thinly
    sliced
½ cup chopped parsley leaves, optional

1 • Place about one-third of the cucumbers in a shallow bowl. Season generously with salt and pepper. Sprinkle about one-third of the onion slices on top of the cucumbers. Make 2 more layers with the remaining cucumbers and onions, remembering to season with salt and pepper as you go.

2 • Drizzle the dressing over the salad, add the parsley, and toss gently. Cover with plastic wrap and refrigerate for up to 3 hours. Serve chilled.

**NOTE:** You don't have to peel the cucumbers. A nice touch is to rake each cucumber lengthwise with the tines of a fork before halving and slicing. This gives a decorative border to each slice.

*Makes 6 servings*

# Sicilian Cauliflower Salad

No, there are no horse heads in this salad . . . just kidding. It's a joke. I did not include this salad just to make a few "Mob" jokes. It's a refreshing salad on a hot summer day and looks great. I mean it: this is a salad you can't refuse. Sorry, I just couldn't help it.

1 large head cauliflower
1 (2-ounce) can flat anchovy fillets
    packed in oil, drained
1 cup packed fresh parsley leaves, plus
    extra for garnish
5 sun-dried tomatoes packed in oil,
    drained

¼ cup drained capers
¼ cup freshly squeezed lemon juice
    (from 1 to 2 lemons)
¼ cup extra-virgin olive oil
¾ teaspoon hot red pepper flakes
1 cup imported olives, such as
    Kalamata, pitted

1 • Trim the green leaves and thickest part of the stem from the cauliflower and discard. Cut the cauliflower into 2- to 3-inch florets.

2 • In a large pot fitted with a vegetable steamer, bring 2 inches of water to a boil. Add the cauliflower florets to the steamer basket, and steam until you can just pierce them with the blade of a knife, about 10 minutes. You want the cauliflower to be pretty firm, so watch carefully, as the florets can become mushy quickly. Drain the cauliflower and transfer to a serving bowl.

3 • While the cauliflower is cooking, combine the anchovies, parsley, sun-dried tomatoes, capers, lemon juice, olive oil, and red pepper flakes in the work bowl of a food processor or in a blender. Process until smooth.

4 • Pour the anchovy mixture over the steamed cauliflower while the florets are still hot. Let the cauliflower marinate for at least 1 hour at room temperature. The salad can be made in advance and covered and refrigerated for up to 4 hours. Bring to room temperature before serving.

5 • Garnish with the olives and some parsley leaves just before serving.

*Makes 8 servings*

# Collards

A staple of southern cooking, collard greens are a must for a real barbecue. These aren't quite as greasy as traditional collards, but they still have plenty of flavor.

3 or 4 bunches collard greens or kale
  (3 to 4 pounds)
1 ham hock
2 medium onions, peeled and chopped
1 head garlic, peeled and chopped

1/2 cup cider vinegar
Salt
Vinegar or hot pepper vinegar,
  for serving

1 • Trim the thickest stems from the greens. Rinse and drain the greens and cut them into 1-inch strips. Put the greens in a very large pot with the ham hock, onions, garlic, cider vinegar, and salt. Cover with cold water by several inches. Cover the pot, set it over high heat, and bring the water to a boil. Reduce the heat to a simmer, and cook for 3 to 4 hours, until the greens are very tender.

2 • Drain and serve hot, with plain or hot pepper vinegar on the side.

*Makes 8 to 10 servings*

# Skillet Corn Bread, Two Ways

A story about corn bread: Before we were married, I invited Deborah and a good friend of ours, Carl Killingsworth, over for dinner. Carl is from North Carolina and Deborah's from Georgia. So I decided I was going to make corn bread in honor of their southern heritage. Unbeknownst to me, Deborah and Carl had conspired to make their own corn bread, using ingredients Carl's mother, Sally, had sent to him.

Deborah gets on the phone to her mom, Ruth, to get the recipe. She dutifully writes it all down, and now she and Carl are ready to make corn bread. I look at the list and I say, "Sweetie, there's no baking powder listed here." Deborah looks at me and says, "I've watched my mother make corn bread for years. I know what goes into it." I reply, "But there's nothing to make the bread rise. Maybe your mom meant for you to use self-rising cornmeal or self-rising flour." She looked at me indignantly and said, "Carl and I are from the South. We know what we're doing."

I said, "You know, just for fun, I'll make some corn bread and we can have a little of both."

Needless to say, their cornbread was about as flat as a pancake, while this good ol' northern boy's corn bread came out nice and fluffy. The South may rise again, but Deborah's corn bread won't.

½ cup canola oil, or other vegetable oil
1½ cups yellow cornmeal
1½ cups all-purpose flour
¼ cup sugar
4½ teaspoons baking powder
2 teaspoons salt
1½ cups half-and-half, or whole milk
2 large eggs

**FOR SPICY CORN BREAD**

4 ounces shredded Monterey Jack
   cheese (1 cup)
⅓ medium red onion, peeled and finely
   chopped
3 jalapeño peppers, stemmed, seeded,
   and finely chopped

1 • Position a rack in the center of the oven and preheat the oven to 450 degrees F.

2 • Pour the oil into a 10-inch, cast-iron skillet and heat it in the oven until almost smoking, 5 to 10 minutes.

3 • Meanwhile, in a large mixing bowl, stir together the cornmeal, flour, sugar, baking powder, and salt.

4 • In a separate bowl, whisk together the half-and-half and eggs. Stir the wet ingredients into the dry ingredients. If making spicy corn bread, add the cheese, onion, and jalapeño peppers.

5 • Remove the skillet from the oven and slowly add the hot oil to the corn-bread mixture, stirring between additions. When all of the oil has been added, spoon the batter into the hot skillet and return the skillet to the oven. Immediately reduce the heat to 400 degrees F and bake for about 25 minutes, until a knife inserted into the center comes out clean.

6 • Remove from the oven, and cool in the pan on a cake rack for 10 minutes. Run a knife around the edge, and turn the corn bread out onto a cake rack. Invert, and serve right side up warm or at room temperature.

*Makes 8 servings*

# Creamed Corn Bread

1 cup yellow cornmeal
1 cup all-purpose flour
¼ cup sugar
1 tablespoon baking powder
½ teaspoon salt

½ cup whole milk
2 large eggs
4 tablespoons (½ stick) unsalted
    butter, melted and cooled
1 (15-ounce) can creamed corn

1 • Position a rack in the center of the oven and preheat the oven to 400 degrees F. Lightly grease an 8-inch round baking pan with sides at least 1½ inches high.

2 • In a large mixing bowl, stir together the cornmeal, flour, sugar, baking powder, and salt.

3 • In a separate bowl, mix together the milk, eggs, melted butter, and creamed corn. Stir this mixture into the dry ingredients and mix just until combined.

4 • Spoon the batter into the prepared pan. Bake for about 30 minutes, until a knife inserted into the center comes out clean.

5 • Remove from the oven, and cool in the pan on a cake rack for 10 minutes. Run a knife around the edge, and turn the corn bread out onto a cake rack. Invert, and serve right side up warm or at room temperature.

*Makes 8 servings*

# The Finish

## A Note on Dessert

I think dessert is one area that is overlooked at a barbecue. Here's a surprise. I like dessert. And I see no reason to skip it just because we're eating outside. Nothing fancy, nothing pretentious. Just good desserts that remind us of childhood and picnics with family and friends.

# Grilled Fruit 101

I maintain there isn't anything that you can't make better by grilling it. Fruit is no exception. We always think of fruit as needing to be served cold. I'm here to tell you that warm, grilled fruit is a nice way to end a meal. It surprises a lot of people, but the surprise turns to appreciation very quickly.

You may want to serve a mixed, grilled fruit plate with a dollop of Classic Vanilla Ice Cream (page 148) and any leftover warm glaze.

## HONEY GLAZE

8 tablespoons (1 stick) unsalted butter, melted
1/4 cup honey

3 tablespoons freshly squeezed lime juice (from 1 to 2 limes)

Stir together all of the ingredients until smooth.

*Makes 1 cup, or enough to coat 3 to 4 pounds of fruit*

### Grilled Bananas

Peel the bananas, and slice each in half crosswise and then lengthwise. (You will have 4 pieces, each about 4 inches long and $1/2$ inch thick.) Add a pinch of ground cinnamon and/or 2 tablespoons of dark rum to the honey glaze. Using a pastry brush, coat the banana pieces with the glaze. Grill over direct medium heat (see pages 11–14) for 6 to 8 minutes, turning gently, until light brown.

### Grilled Peaches, Nectarines, Plums

Halve the fruit and remove the pits. Toss the fruit gently in a bowl with the honey glaze. Grill, cut side down, over direct medium heat (see pages 11–14) for 10 to 12 minutes, turning after 7 to 8 minutes.

### Grilled Pineapple

Cut off the top and the peel. Slice the fruit into $3/4$-inch-thick rounds. Add 2 tablespoons of dark rum to the honey glaze. Using a pastry brush, coat both sides of each slice with the glaze. Grill over direct medium heat (see pages 11–14) for 12 to 15 minutes, turning once halfway through.

# Mango-Melon-Berry Salad

The tangy dressing works well with many kinds of fruits. Use any combination that suits you, such as grapes, pears, pineapple, or strawberries; try adding an apple for crispness.

## FOR THE DRESSING

1 cup water
2/3 cup sugar
1/3 cup sherry vinegar

1 tablespoon freshly squeezed orange juice

1 • In a small saucepan set over medium-high heat, combine all of the ingredients and bring to a boil. Reduce the heat to a simmer and cook, uncovered, until the syrup lightly coats the back of the spoon. This will take about 15 minutes, at which point you will have about 1/2 cup of dressing. Remove from the heat and cool to room temperature.

2 • Use immediately or cover and store, refrigerated, for up to 4 days.

## FOR THE SALAD

1 large mango
1/2 large cantaloupe, halved and seeded
2 1/2 cups raspberries (15 ounces), picked over, rinsed, and drained

2 cups blueberries (12 ounces), picked over, rinsed, and drained
1/3 cup chopped mint leaves

1 • Peel the mango by making 4 lengthwise incisions in the skin with a sharp knife, then pulling off the skin. Working on a cutting board with a sharp knife, slice the flesh away from the pit. Chop the flesh and place it in a serving bowl.

2 • Cut the cantaloupe off the rind into bite-sized pieces. Add to the serving bowl, along with the raspberries, blueberries, and mint. Drizzle the fruit with the dressing. Serve immediately or cover and refrigerate for up to 6 hours.

*Makes 6 servings*

# Raspberry Citrus Ice

How easy is this? We all know how to make ice, right? Water . . . really cold temperatures . . . BAM . . . you've got ice. Well, just add a couple more ingredients and you have a refreshing dessert, perfect for a summer day. You don't need an ice cream maker to make great ice. You *do* need to start the day before you are going to serve it.

1¹/₂ cups water
1 cup sugar
Zest of 1 lemon, removed in wide strips
   with a vegetable peeler
2 cups raspberries (12 ounces), picked
   over, rinsed, and drained
1 tablespoon finely grated orange zest
   (from 1 orange)

1¹/₂ cups freshly squeezed orange juice
   (from 4 oranges)
¹/₄ cup freshly squeezed lemon juice
   (from 1 to 2 lemons)
1 tablespoon orange-flavored liqueur,
   optional

1 • The night before you are planning to serve the ice, combine the water, sugar, and lemon zest in a saucepan set over medium-high heat. Bring to a boil, lower the heat, and simmer, stirring occasionally, for 5 minutes. Remove from the heat and cool to room temperature.

2 • Strain the cooled syrup into an 8-inch, non-reactive baking pan with sides at least 1¹/₂ inches high, or a large plastic container. Discard the lemon zest. Add the raspberries, orange zest, orange and lemon juices, and liqueur (if using), and stir to mix well. Cover and freeze overnight.

3 • The next morning, chop the ice into chunks and, working in batches if necessary, puree in the work bowl of a food processor until smooth. Place in a lidded plastic container, cover, and freeze for at least 5 hours or up to 1 week.

4 • Scoop into serving bowls, preferably glass, to show off the color of the ice.

*Makes about 5 cups, or 6 servings*

# Watermelon Ice

3/4 cup sugar
1/2 cup water
Zest of 1 lemon, removed in wide strips
    with a vegetable peeler
Zest of 1 lime, removed in wide strips
    with a vegetable peeler
About 4 cups 2-inch chunks seeded
    watermelon (from a 3-pound piece
    of melon)

1/3 cup freshly squeezed lemon juice
    (from 2 lemons)
2 tablespoons raspberry liqueur
Mint leaves for garnish, optional

1 • In a small saucepan set over medium-high heat, combine the sugar, water, and lemon and lime zests. Bring to a boil, lower the heat, and simmer, stirring occasionally, for 5 minutes. Remove from the heat and cool to room temperature. Strain the cooled syrup into an 8-inch, non-reactive baking pan with sides at least 1 1/2 inches high, or a large plastic container. Discard the zest.

2 • Puree the watermelon in batches in the work bowl of a food processor or in a blender. You need 2 1/2 cups of pureed melon.

3 • Stir the watermelon puree into the sugar syrup, then stir in the lemon juice and the liqueur. Cover and freeze overnight.

4 • The next morning, chop the ice into chunks and, working in batches if necessary, puree in the work bowl of a food processor until smooth. Place in a lidded plastic container, cover, and freeze for at least 5 hours and up to 1 week.

5 • Scoop into serving bowls, preferably glass, to show off the color of the ice, and garnish with fresh mint leaves, if desired, before serving.

*Makes 4 cups, or 4 servings*

# Fudgy Brownies

Look, you can put nuts in your brownies. Me, I like my food groups separate. Chocolate and nuts don't go together. I like brownies as brown as possible, without pieces of nuts to get in the way.

8 ounces unsweetened chocolate, finely
    chopped
12 tablespoons (1½ sticks) unsalted
    butter
2½ cups sugar

½ cup corn syrup
4 large eggs, lightly beaten
1 tablespoon pure vanilla extract
½ teaspoon salt
1½ cups all-purpose flour

1 • Position a rack in the center of the oven and preheat the oven to 350 degrees F. Grease and flour a 9 by 13-inch baking pan with sides at least 1½ inches high.

2 • In a heavy-bottomed, large saucepan set over very low heat, melt the chocolate and butter stirring to mix. Remove the saucepan from the heat, and stir in the sugar, corn syrup, eggs, and vanilla. Add the salt and stir to mix well. Add the flour and mix just until combined.

3 • Spread the batter in the prepared pan and bake for about 35 minutes, or until a knife inserted in the middle comes out with just a few crumbs attached (not wet, but not perfectly dry).

4 • Cool in the pan on a cake rack. Cut into 2-inch squares and serve plain, or, for a brownie sundae, serve with Classic Vanilla Ice Cream (page 148) and hot fudge, butterscotch, or raspberry sauce (pages 152–154).

*Makes 24 brownies*

## Variations

**Mocha Brownies:** Add 3 tablespoons of instant espresso when you add the flour.

**Nut Brownies:** Like I said, if you wanna . . . go nuts. Just don't bring these to my house. Stir in 1 cup of nuts (walnuts, pecans, or almonds) after all of the other ingredients have been added. For even better flavor, toast the nuts first (page 97).

**No-Fuss Frosted Brownies:** After you remove the pan from the oven, let it sit for 2 to 3 minutes. Sprinkle $1^1/_2$ cups semisweet chocolate chips evenly over the top. Return the pan to the oven for 2 minutes, remove, then spread the chocolate frosting.

# Blueberry Cobbler

I am a big fan of the cobbler. I like apple cobbler but always feel like it's just apple pie that went wrong. But the colors of a blueberry cobbler are wonderful. The brown and tan of the crust, the purple-blue of the berries all sitting there, waiting. American as apple pie . . . I don't think so.

## FOR THE FILLING

4 cups blueberries (24 ounces), picked
    over, rinsed, and drained
1/2 cup sugar
1 1/2 teaspoons finely grated orange zest
    (from 1 orange)

1/4 cup freshly squeezed orange juice
    (from 1 orange)
1/4 teaspoon ground cinnamon
Large pinch of ground nutmeg

1 • Position a rack in the center of the oven, and preheat the oven to 375 degrees F.
2 • Mix all of the filling ingredients gently in a bowl. Let sit at room temperature for 15 minutes. Spoon into a 9-inch pie plate or quiche pan, then place the pan on a baking sheet. Bake until the fruit begins to bubble, about 10 minutes. While the fruit is in the oven, make the topping.

## FOR THE TOPPING

1 1/2 cups all-purpose flour
1/4 cup sugar
2 teaspoons baking powder
2 teaspoons baking soda
1 1/2 teaspoons finely grated orange zest
    (from 1 orange)

1/4 teaspoon salt
5 tablespoons unsalted butter, chilled
1 cup buttermilk

1 • In the work bowl of a food processor or in a mixing bowl, blend together the flour, sugar, baking powder, baking soda, orange zest, and salt. *If using a food processor,* add the butter and pulse until dry and crumbly. *If mixing by hand,* cut the butter into the flour mixture with a pastry cutter or 2 knives until crumbly. Add the buttermilk, and mix just until a soft dough forms. Do not overmix.

2 • When the fruit is bubbling, remove the pie pan from the oven and cover the top with heaping tablespoonfuls of batter. (The batter will spread during baking to form a complete crust.) Return the pan to the oven and bake until lightly browned, about 30 minutes, or until the center is no longer doughy (poke it with a knife to check). Remove from the oven and cool, at least slightly, on a cake rack. Serve warm or at room temperature, either plain or with Classic Vanilla Ice Cream (page 148) or whipped cream.

*Makes 8 servings*

# Peach Pie

Since barbecue is considered a southern art form, I should include a southern dessert. My wife is from Georgia, and the state fruit makes a darn tasty pie.

**FOR THE CRUST**

| | |
|---|---|
| 8 tablespoons (1 stick) unsalted butter, at room temperature | 1 teaspoon almond extract |
| | 2¹/₂ cups all-purpose flour |
| ³/₄ cup sugar | 1 teaspoon baking powder |
| 1 large egg | ¹/₂ teaspoon salt |
| 2 large egg yolks | |

1 • In the bowl of an electric mixer or in a large bowl, combine the butter and sugar. In a separate bowl, whisk together the egg, egg yolks, and almond extract. Add the egg mixture to the butter mixture and mix until smooth.

2 • In another bowl, stir together the flour, baking powder, and salt. Add the dry ingredients to the butter mixture and mix just until a dough forms. Pinch off about one-third of the dough, wrap it in plastic wrap, and refrigerate. Press the remaining two-thirds of the dough into a 9-inch pie plate. It should make a ¹/₄-inch-thick crust. Refrigerate the crust while you make the filling.

**FOR THE FILLING**

| | |
|---|---|
| 6 medium peaches (2¹/₄ pounds), pitted and sliced | ³/₄ cup sugar |
| | 1 teaspoon almond extract |

1 • In a medium saucepan set over medium-low heat, combine the peaches, sugar, and almond extract. Cook, stirring occasionally, for about 20 minutes, until the peaches are soft. Remove from the heat and cool to room temperature.

2 • Center a rack in the oven and preheat the oven to 350 degrees F.

3 • Pour the cooled peach filling into the chilled pastry shell.

4 • Roll out the remaining third of the dough on a well-floured surface to form a 10-inch circle. Cut the dough into 6 to 8 strips, each 1 inch wide, and lay half of the strips on top of the filling, at regular intervals. Crisscross the remaining strips on top of the first layer to make a lattice crust. Pinch together the edges of the bottom crust and the lattice strips. Cover the edge of the crust with aluminum foil to prevent it from burning, and bake for about 40 minutes, until the top is golden and the peaches are bubbling.

5 • Cut the pie into 8 slices, and serve warm or at room temperature, topping each slice with Classic Vanilla Ice Cream (page 148), if desired.

*Makes 8 servings*

# Berry Shortcake with Vanilla Whipped Cream

You should always take advantage of the flavors of the season, and strawberries are synonymous with summer. Fresh strawberries, in a dish with a sprinkling of sugar, are hard to beat. But you know, I have to try.

### FOR THE BISCUIT

| | |
|---|---|
| 3 cups all-purpose flour | 1/2 teaspoon salt |
| 1/4 cup sugar | 8 tablespoons (1 stick) unsalted butter, |
| 1 tablespoon baking powder | chilled |
| 1 1/2 teaspoons baking soda | 1 cup buttermilk |

1 • Position a rack in the center of the oven and preheat the oven to 400 degrees F. Grease an 8 1/2- or 9-inch springform pan, or a 9-inch cake pan with sides at least 1 1/2 inches high.

2 • In the work bowl of a food processor or in a mixing bowl, combine the flour, sugar, baking powder, baking soda, and salt and mix well. *If using a food processor,* add the butter and pulse until the mixture resembles dry bread crumbs. *If mixing by hand,* cut in the butter with a pastry cutter or 2 knives until crumbly. Add the buttermilk, and mix just until a dough forms. Do not overmix.

3 • Press the dough evenly into the prepared pan. Bake for 15 to 20 minutes, until the top is a light golden color and a knife inserted in the center comes out clean. Remove from the oven, and cool in the pan on a cake rack. When the biscuit is cool, run a knife around the edge, and turn the biscuit out of the pan. You can make the biscuit a day ahead of time. Wrap it tightly in plastic wrap and store at room temperature.

| | |
|---|---|
| 8 cups strawberries (2 pounds), or other berries such as blueberries or raspberries, or a combination | 2 cups heavy cream, chilled |
| | 2 tablespoons sugar |
| | 2 teaspoons pure vanilla extract |
| 1/4 cup thawed frozen orange juice concentrate | |

1 • Up to 2 hours before serving, prepare the fruit. Pick over all of the berries, discarding any bruised or unripe fruit. Rinse and drain the berries. If using strawberries, hull them. If using blueberries, remove any stems.

2 • Smash the berries lightly with a potato masher or fork and stir in the orange juice concentrate. Let sit at room temperature for at least 30 minutes.

3 • No more than 30 minutes before serving, whip the cream. When soft peaks form, add the sugar and the vanilla. Continue whipping until stiff peaks form.

4 • Using a sharp, serrated knife, slice the biscuit in half horizontally and put the bottom half on a cake plate. Spoon about two-thirds of the berries over the biscuit and top with half of the whipped cream. Top with the remaining biscuit half and cover with the remaining whipped cream. Spoon the remaining berries on top, allowing some cream and berries to ooze down the sides. Serve within 30 minutes, cutting the shortcake into 8 slices.

*Makes 8 servings*

# Rustic Blackberry Tart

You can make this with any kind of berry. Pick a fruit preserve that will match or complement your choice of berry.

## FOR THE CRUST

1 unbaked, store-bought, refrigerated
    single (9-inch) pie crust
or
1⅓ cups all-purpose flour
¼ teaspoon salt

6 tablespoons (¾ stick) unsalted
    butter, chilled
2 to 3 tablespoons very cold water

1 • *If making your own pie crust,* put the flour and salt in the work bowl of a food processor or in a large mixing bowl. *If using a food processor,* add the butter and pulse until the mixture forms pea-sized crumbs. *If mixing by hand,* cut in the butter with a pastry cutter or 2 knives. Add 2 tablespoons of very cold water, and mix just until a dough forms, with no crumbs in the bottom of the bowl or food processor work bowl. If you need more water, add the last tablespoon 1 teaspoon at a time, so that you don't put in too much. Do not overmix. Gather the dough into a ball, wrap it in plastic wrap, and refrigerate for at least 1 hour or overnight.

2 • Lightly grease a baking sheet and set it aside.

3 • Whether you are using a store-bought crust or a homemade one, roll the dough with a floured rolling pin on a floured work surface to make a 13- or 14-inch circle. Keep moving and flouring the dough as you roll so that it does not stick to the work surface. Transfer the crust to the prepared baking sheet and refrigerate for 30 minutes.

## FOR THE FILLING

4 cups fresh blackberries (24 ounces),
   picked over, rinsed, and drained

¹/₄ cup sugar
2 tablespoons instant tapioca

Toss the berries with the sugar and tapioca, and let sit at room temperature while the crust is chilling.

## TO BAKE

1 large egg yolk, lightly beaten
1 cup blackberry or raspberry preserves

1 large egg white, lightly beaten

1 • Position a rack in the center of the oven and preheat the oven to 400 degrees F.

2 • Remove the dough from the refrigerator and, using a pastry brush, brush it with the egg yolk, leaving a 2- to 3-inch border unglazed around the edge. The glaze helps to keep the dough from leaking. Discard any excess egg yolk.

3 • Spread the preserves over the circle of dough that has been glazed with the egg yolk. Spoon the berries on top. Turn up the unglazed border of the dough around the fruit, pleating the edges as necessary to form a rough circle. Brush the exposed dough border with the egg white. Discard any excess egg white.

4 • Bake for about 35 minutes, or until the fruit is bubbling and the crust is golden. Serve warm or at room temperature, either plain, or with Classic Vanilla Ice Cream (page 148) or whipped cream.

*Makes 8 servings*

# Margarita Pie

You can salt the rim of the pie pan, but I think that's taking the margarita thing a bit too far.

**FOR THE CRUST**

| | |
|---|---|
| 1 store-bought (9-inch) graham cracker crust <br><br> or | 1½ cups graham cracker crumbs <br> 6 tablespoons (¾ stick) unsalted butter, melted |

1 • *If making the crust,* position a rack in the center of the oven and preheat the oven to 350 degrees F.
2 • In a medium bowl, mix together the cookie crumbs and butter. Press into a 9-inch pie plate. Bake until the crust starts to puff up a bit, about 8 minutes. Remove from the oven. If the crust has shrunk from the sides of the pan, use the back of a spoon to press it out to the edges again. Remove from the oven, and cool completely on a cake rack.

**FOR THE FILLING**

| | |
|---|---|
| 1 (14-ounce) can sweetened condensed milk <br> 1 tablespoon finely grated lime zest (from 2 to 3 limes) <br> 6 tablespoons freshly squeezed lime juice (from 3 limes) | 3 tablespoons tequila <br> 2 teaspoons orange-flavored liqueur <br> Pinch of salt |

1 • Stir together all of the ingredients. Let sit for about 5 minutes to thicken.
2 • Pour the filling into the cooled crust. Cover with plastic wrap and refrigerate until firmly set, at least 2 hours or up to 8 hours.

> *1 cup heavy cream, chilled*
> *1 tablespoon sugar*
>
> *1 teaspoon pure vanilla extract*
> *Lime slices, optional*

1 • Just before serving, whip the cream. When soft peaks form, add the sugar and the vanilla. Continue whipping until stiff peaks form.

2 • Garnish the chilled pie with the whipped cream and lime slices (if using) and serve.

*Makes 8 servings*

# Make-Your-Own Ice Cream Pie

Here's where you can take something homemade, combine it with something you buy off the shelf, and come up with a fabulous dessert.

**FOR THE CRUST**

1 store-bought (9-inch) graham cracker
   crust
or
1¹/₂ cups chocolate wafer crumbs
   (25 to 30 wafers)

¹/₂ teaspoon ground cinnamon
6 tablespoons (³/₄ stick) unsalted
   butter, melted

1 • *If making the crust,* position a rack in the center of the oven and preheat the oven to 350 degrees F.

2 • In a medium bowl, mix together the cookie crumbs, cinnamon, and melted butter. Press into a 9-inch pie plate. Bake until the crust begins to puff up a bit, about 8 minutes. If the crust has shrunk from the sides of the pan, use the back of a spoon to press it out to the edges again. Remove from the oven, and cool completely on a cake rack.

**FOR THE FILLING**

¹/₂ recipe Classic Vanilla Ice Cream with mix-ins (pages 148–149), or 2 cups (1 pint) store-
   bought ice cream of your choice

1 • Spoon the ice cream into the crust. (You can soften the ice cream by warming it in a microwave on high for about 15 seconds or by putting it in the refrigerator for about 30 minutes.) Using a flat metal spatula or a butter knife, smooth the top of the ice cream so it is even.

2 • Wrap in plastic wrap and freeze for at least 2 hours or for up to 3 days. Unwrap and cut into 8 slices with a knife that has been dipped in hot water, re-dipping before cutting each additional slice.

3 • Serve as is, or topped with whipped cream and Hot Fudge Sauce (page 152) or Butterscotch Sauce (page 153).

*Makes 8 servings*

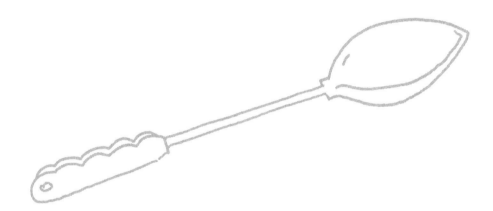

# Peanut Butter–Chocolate Chip Cookie Ice Cream Sandwiches

This is what I love. Taking something that we all remember from our childhood and turning it into something just a little more special. You can fill any of your favorite cookies with ice cream for your own homemade ice cream sandwich. These are best made a day ahead.

**FOR THE PEANUT BUTTER–CHOCOLATE CHIP COOKIES**

5 tablespoons unsalted butter, at room
    temperature
1/2 cup packed dark brown sugar
1/4 cup sugar
2 teaspoons corn syrup
2/3 cup creamy peanut butter
1 large egg
1 teaspoon pure vanilla extract

1 cup plus 2 tablespoons all-purpose
    flour
1/2 teaspoon baking soda
1/4 teaspoon salt
6 ounces semisweet chocolate, cut into
    chunks, or 1 cup semisweet
    chocolate chips

1 • Position a rack in the center of the oven and preheat the oven to 375 degrees F.

2 • In the bowl of an electric mixer or in a large bowl, mix together the butter, brown sugar, sugar, corn syrup, and peanut butter. Add the egg and the vanilla and mix well. In a separate bowl, stir together the flour, baking soda, and salt. Add these dry ingredients to the dough and mix just until combined. Stir in the chocolate chunks by hand.

3 • Measure out 2 tablespoons of the dough and roll into a ball. Repeat with the remaining dough. This will give you 16 cookies, each 3 1/2 inches in diameter, or enough for 8 ice cream sandwiches. Place each ball on an ungreased baking sheet and flatten with the bottom of a glass dipped in flour to make a 1/4-inch-thick disk.

4 • Bake for 9 to 12 minutes, until the cookies are lightly browned.

5 • Remove the cookies from the oven, and leave them on the baking sheet for 2 to 3 min-

utes. Using a metal spatula, carefully remove the cookies from the baking sheet and place on a cake rack to cool completely. You can make the cookies a day ahead of time and keep them in an airtight container.

## TO ASSEMBLE

*Classic Vanilla Ice Cream (page 148), or about 3 cups (1½ pints) store-bought ice cream of your choice*

Make the ice cream sandwiches at least 1 to 2 hours before serving. Working very quickly, scoop ¹/₄ to ¹/₃ cup of ice cream (about an average ice cream scoop) onto the underside of a cookie. (You can soften the ice cream by warming it in a microwave on high for about 15 seconds or by putting it in the refrigerator for about 30 minutes.) Put another cookie—flat side against the ice cream—on top and press gently so that the ice cream spreads evenly to the edges. The filling will be ¹/₂ to ³/₄ inch thick. Wrap the filled cookies in plastic wrap and freeze until hard, at least 1 hour or up to 1 week.

*Makes 8 sandwiches*

# Classic Vanilla Ice Cream

One of my favorite desserts is good quality plain ol' vanilla ice cream. I love ice cream, and this is another example of time well spent. Your guests will taste the difference and they'll appreciate it. If you become really good at it, get a partner named Ben and move to Vermont . . .

Try this with a hot fudge, butterscotch, or raspberry sauce (pages 152–154), Fudgy Brownies (page 132), or any of the mix-ins (see page 149).

---

| | |
|---|---|
| 6 large egg yolks | 1 cup whole milk |
| 2/3 cup sugar | 1 (4- to 5-inch long) vanilla bean, or |
| 2 cups heavy cream | 2 tablespoons pure vanilla extract |

---

1 • In a medium mixing bowl, whisk together the egg yolks and sugar until thoroughly blended. Set aside.

2 • Fill a large bowl halfway with ice and cold water. Set out a smaller bowl (with a minimum capacity of 1¹/₂ quarts) that will fit inside the larger bowl.

3 • Bring about 2 inches of water to a simmer in the bottom of a double boiler. Put the cream and milk in the top pan of the double boiler, off the heat. If using the vanilla bean, cut it in half lengthwise with a small, sharp knife. Using the tip of the knife, scrape the inside of the bean into the cream mixture, then put the bean itself into the mixture. (If using vanilla extract, do not add it now.) Set the top pan of the double boiler over the simmering water, and heat the cream mixture until bubbles just begin to form around the edges. Do not let the mixture boil.

4 • Slowly add about 1 cup of the hot cream to the egg yolk mixture, whisking briskly to combine. Stir the yolk mixture into the remaining cream in the double boiler and whisk well. Cook over simmering water, stirring constantly with a stainless steel or wooden spoon, until the mixture thickens slightly and coats the back of the spoon, about 5 minutes. Remove from the heat and immediately pour the mixture into the smaller bowl that you have set out. Place this bowl in the prepared ice water bath. Stir to cool the mixture.

5 • When the ice cream base is cool, remove the vanilla bean. If using vanilla extract instead, stir it in now. Cover and refrigerate until thoroughly chilled, at least 1 hour or overnight.

6 • Freeze the chilled mixture in an ice cream maker, following the manufacturer's instructions, adding any mix-ins (see below) as directed. Depending on the ice cream maker, the ice cream will probably be very soft when done. You can serve the ice cream immediately, or pack it into an airtight plastic container and freeze it until firm, 3 to 4 hours. It will keep for several weeks in the freezer.

*Makes about 5 cups, or 10 servings*

## Mix-Ins

*Add any of the following (about ¹/₂ cup total per recipe) in any combination, following the manufacturer's directions. You can also add these (about ¹/₃ cup per quart) to softened, store-bought ice cream. Possible mix-ins include: candy-coated chocolates, mini or regular chocolate chips, crushed chocolate sandwich cookies, chopped chocolate-covered peanut butter cups, crushed peppermint candies, toasted nuts (see page 97), or chopped toffee bars.*

# Perfect Peach Ice Cream

I dedicate this to my own little Georgia Peach, Deborah.

---

3 large egg yolks
3/4 cup sugar
2 cups heavy cream
1/2 cup whole milk

5 medium peaches (1 3/4 pounds)
3/4 teaspoon almond extract

---

1 • In a medium bowl, whisk together the egg yolks and 1/2 cup of the sugar. Set aside.

2 • Fill a large bowl halfway with ice and cold water. Set out a smaller bowl (with a minimum capacity of 2 quarts) that will fit inside the larger bowl.

3 • Bring about 2 inches of water to a simmer in the bottom of a double boiler. Put the cream and milk in the top pan of the double boiler, and heat until bubbles just begin to form around the edges. Do not let the mixture boil.

4 • Slowly add about 1 cup of the hot cream to the egg yolk mixture, whisking briskly to combine. Stir the yolk mixture into the remaining cream in the double boiler and whisk well. Cook over simmering water, stirring constantly with a stainless steel or wooden spoon, until the mixture thickens slightly and coats the back of the spoon, about 5 minutes. Remove from the heat and immediately pour the mixture into the smaller bowl that you have set out. Place this bowl in the prepared ice water bath. Stir to cool the mixture.

5 • When the ice cream base is cool, cover and refrigerate it until thoroughly chilled, at least 1 hour or overnight.

6 • Bring a pot of water to a boil. Plunge the peaches into the boiling water for 1 minute, remove with a slotted spoon, and, when cool enough to handle, slip off the peels. Cut the peaches in half, remove the pits, and cut the fruit into 1/4-inch pieces. You should have about 2 cups of fruit.

7 • Sprinkle the peaches with the remaining 1/4 cup of sugar and the almond extract. Let the peaches sit for at least 30 minutes at room temperature for the flavors to blend.

8 • Puree half of the peaches in the work bowl of a food processor or in a blender. Stir the peach puree into the chilled ice cream base. Then stir in the remaining peach chunks.

9 • Freeze the mixture in an ice cream maker, following the manufacturer's instructions. Depending on the ice cream maker, the ice cream will probably be very soft when done. You can serve it immediately, or pack it into an airtight plastic container and freeze it until firm, 3 to 4 hours. It will keep for several weeks in the freezer.

**VARIATIONS:** For strawberry ice cream, substitute pure vanilla extract for the almond extract, and 1 pint hulled, chopped, strawberries for the chopped peaches.

*Makes 6 cups, or 12 servings*

## Homemade Ice Cream

*When making ice cream at home, remember to plan ahead: you may need to freeze a component of your ice cream maker overnight; you need time for the ice cream base to chill before churning it into ice cream; and you need time for the finished product to freeze. Making the base a day ahead is always a good idea.*

# Hot Fudge Sauce

4 tablespoons (¹/₂ stick) unsalted
   butter
³/₄ cup heavy cream
6 tablespoons light corn syrup
1¹/₂ cups sugar

8 ounces unsweetened chocolate, finely
   chopped
³/₄ cup boiling water
1 tablespoon pure vanilla extract
Pinch of salt

1 • In a medium saucepan set over low heat, melt the butter. Add the heavy cream, corn syrup, sugar, and chocolate and stir until the chocolate is melted and the sugar is almost dissolved, 5 to 7 minutes.

2 • Bring the mixture to a simmer. Add the boiling water and briefly stir to combine. Cook over medium heat for 5 minutes without stirring.

3 • Remove from the heat, stir in the vanilla and salt, and let cool slightly. Use immediately or cover and store in a heatproof jar in the refrigerator for up to 1 week.

4 • Serve the sauce warm over ice cream. If the sauce was refrigerated, reheat the jar of sauce in a saucepan of simmering water, stirring occasionally, until the sauce is heated through. The sauce can also be reheated in the microwave (make sure to remove any metal lids). Warm at half power for about 2 minutes, stirring halfway through.

*Makes 3¹/₂ cups*

# Butterscotch Sauce

3/4 cup packed light brown sugar
1/4 cup light corn syrup
1/4 cup water
1 cup heavy cream, warm

3 tablespoons unsalted butter
1/2 teaspoon pure vanilla extract
Pinch of salt

1 • In a heavy-bottomed saucepan set over medium heat, combine the sugar, corn syrup, and water. Cook, stirring constantly, until the sugar has dissolved and the water has nearly evaporated, 8 to 10 minutes. Carefully add the cream and stir to combine. Add the butter and stir until melted. Remove from the heat and stir in the vanilla and salt.

2 • Use immediately or cover and store in a heatproof jar in the refrigerator for up to 1 week.

3 • Serve the sauce warm over ice cream. If the sauce was refrigerated, reheat the jar of sauce in a saucepan of simmering water, stirring occasionally, until the sauce is heated through. The sauce can also be reheated in the microwave (make sure to remove any metal lids). Warm at half power for about 2 minutes, stirring halfway through.

*Makes about 2 cups*

# Raspberry Sauce

¼ cup water
½ cup sugar
Zest of one lemon, removed in wide
    strips with a vegetable peeler

2½ cups fresh raspberries (15 ounces),
    picked over, rinsed, and drained

1 • Combine the water, sugar, and lemon zest in a small saucepan. Bring to a boil, lower the heat, and simmer, stirring occasionally, for 5 minutes. Remove from the heat, and cool to room temperature. Remove the zest.

2 • Combine the sugar syrup and raspberries in the work bowl of a food processor or in a blender. Puree until smooth. Strain through a sieve to remove the seeds, if desired.

3 • Serve immediately or cover and refrigerate for up to 2 days.

*Makes 1½ cups*

# Drinks

## A Note on Drinks

I'm going to be honest with you. When it comes to alcoholic drinks, I really am not much of an imbiber. I may have the occasional margarita or sangría, maybe a piña colada, but that's about it. That's why only one beverage in this book has alcohol in it. You could certainly make Frozen Watermelon Daiquiris (page 162) without the rum. Or, conversely, you could spike all the others if so inclined.

Actually, on a hot day, the last thing you want to drink is an alcoholic beverage. The alcohol opens up your blood vessels, bringing your blood to the surface of your skin. Since it's hot out, you're just warming up your blood. But before you start throwing things at me, I will allow that there's something about a nice drink or two before, during, and after a family barbecue.

That said, please indulge responsibly and if you don't, make sure there's a designated driver. We want you back next grilling season to make a fool of yourself in front of family, friends, and a few strangers who are glad they don't really know you.

# Pretty Pink Punch

This is great as is, but you can also use it as a base for a champagne punch, or for a punch made with light rum or vodka.

1 cup water
1/2 cup sugar
1 cup raspberries (6 ounces), picked over, rinsed, and drained, plus extra for garnish, if desired
2 1/2 cups pineapple juice, chilled
2 cups orange juice, preferably freshly squeezed (from 6 oranges), chilled

2 cups seltzer, chilled
2 cups lemon-lime soda
1 1/4 cups grapefruit juice, chilled
1/4 cup freshly squeezed lemon juice (from 1 to 2 lemons)
Ice, for serving

1 • In a small saucepan set over medium heat, combine the water and sugar. Bring to a boil, lower the heat, and simmer, stirring occasionally, for 5 minutes. Remove from the heat and cool to room temperature.

2 • Push the raspberries through a sieve (to remove the seeds) into the sugar syrup. Discard the seeds. Cover the raspberry mixture and refrigerate until well chilled or for up to 2 days.

3 • Just before serving, combine the raspberry mixture with the pineapple juice, orange juice, seltzer, lemon-lime soda, grapefruit juice, and lemon juice in a 4-quart container or a small punch bowl, stirring gently to combine.

4 • Serve over ice, and garnish with raspberries, if desired.

*Makes about 3 quarts, or 12 servings*

# Lemon-Lime Fizz

1 cup sugar
1/2 cup water
Zest of 1 lemon, removed in wide strips
    with a vegetable peeler
Zest of 1 lime, removed in wide strips
    with a vegetable peeler
2 liters seltzer, chilled

1/2 cup freshly squeezed lemon juice
    (from 2 to 3 lemons)
3 tablespoons freshly squeezed lime
    juice (from 1 to 2 limes)
Ice, for serving
Mint sprigs, and lemon and lime slices,
    for garnish

1 • In a small saucepan set over medium heat, combine the water, sugar, and lemon and lime zests. Bring to a boil, lower the heat, and simmer, stirring occasionally, for 5 minutes. Remove from the heat and cool to room temperature. Remove and discard the zest. Cover the syrup and refrigerate until thoroughly chilled or for up to 2 days.

2 • Just before serving, combine the sugar syrup, seltzer, lemon juice, and lime juice in a 3- or 4-quart pitcher. Serve over ice in tall glasses, and garnish with mint sprigs, and lemon and lime slices, if desired.

*Makes 2 1/2 quarts, or 10 servings*

# Plain and Fancy Lemonade and Iced Tea

### BASIC LEMONADE

2/3 cup sugar
1 cup boiling water
5 cups cold water

3/4 cup freshly squeezed lemon juice
(from 3 lemons)
Ice, for serving

Place the sugar in a heatproof, 2-quart pitcher and pour the boiling water over it. Stir to dissolve the sugar. Stir in the cold water and lemon juice. Serve over ice.

*Makes 1 1/2 quarts, or 6 servings*

### BASIC ICED TEA

6 tea bags, regular, decaf, or herbal
4 cups boiling water

Ice, for serving

Put the teabags in a heatproof pitcher and pour the boiling water over them. Let steep for 5 minutes and then discard the tea bags. When the tea is cool, cover and chill. Serve over ice.

*Makes 1 quart, or 4 servings*

## Variations

**Mint Lemonade:** Add a small handful of fresh mint leaves to the pitcher with the sugar, then add the boiling water. Let steep for at least 5 minutes. Remove and discard the mint leaves and add the remaining ingredients. When serving, garnish with fresh mint leaves.

**Pink Lemonade:** Add 3 tablespoons of grenadine syrup to each quart of lemonade.

**Raspberry Lemonade or Iced Tea:** Boil $1/2$ cup water and $1/2$ cup sugar together for several minutes until the sugar is dissolved. Remove from the heat and cool to room temperature. Puree in a blender 1 cup fresh or frozen raspberries with the syrup. Cover and refrigerate until chilled. Add 1 to 2 tablespoons of the raspberry puree to each 8-ounce glass of lemonade or iced tea. (This is especially good in iced tea made with mint tea bags.)

**Herbed Iced Tea:** Put the tea bags and several sprigs of fresh rosemary and/or thyme in a container and add the boiling water. Discard the herbs when you discard the tea bags. (This is especially good in iced tea made with ginger tea bags.)

**Lemonade Tea:** Add $1/2$ cup iced black or mint tea to each cup of lemonade.

# Frozen Watermelon Daiquiris

| | |
|---|---|
| 4 cups 1-inch chunks seedless water-melon (from a 3-pound piece of melon) | 1/4 cup freshly squeezed lime juice (from 2 limes) |
| 1/2 cup light rum | 2 to 4 tablespoons sugar |
| | Mint leaves, for garnish |

1 • Up to 1 week before you are going to serve the drinks, freeze the watermelon chunks in a single layer on a cookie sheet. When the chunks are frozen, put them into a plastic freezer bag and keep in the freezer until needed or for up to 1 week.

2 • When ready to serve, put the watermelon chunks in the work bowl of a food processor or in a blender. (You will have to work in batches.) Add the rum, lime juice, and 2 table-spoons of the sugar. Taste and add some or all of the remaining 2 tablespoons sugar, if needed.

3 • Pour into chilled glasses and garnish with mint leaves.

*Makes 4 servings*

# Marinades, Rubs, Sauces, and Dressings

## A Note on Marinades

I like marinades for their convenience—they are easy to make, and they do all the work of flavoring and tenderizing the meat by themselves. For this reason, I like a marinade that works overnight, or all day while I'm at work. Most meats can take nearly 24 hours of marinating, which means you can put them in the marinade one night and grill them the next. Poultry can be marinated all day and grilled in the evening. There are a few exceptions in this book, and one of them is seafood, which should only be marinated for 1 to 2 hours, or it will begin to cook from the acid in the marinade and will fall apart on the grill.

Always use a non-reactive (non-aluminum) pan for marinating. Aluminum will discolor when it comes into contact with the acid in the marinade—vinegar, lemon juice, or what have you—and can impart an off taste to the food. A 9 by 13-inch glass or ceramic baking dish usually works nicely, as do glass bowls. For many foods, you can also use a sturdy, plastic food storage bag, which takes up a lot less room in the refrigerator, and makes cleanup easy—just throw away the bag.

When it comes to quantity, less is more. These are intensely flavored marinades, and the food does not have to swim in them. A shallow bath works well; remember to turn the meat, poultry, or fish at least once during the marinating time.

# Asian Marinade

An excellent marinade for London Broil (page 48); also good for chicken, pork, shrimp, or vegetables.

6 cloves garlic, peeled and chopped
5 tablespoons freshly squeezed orange
    juice (from 1 orange)
1/4 cup peanut oil
2 tablespoons peeled, chopped fresh
    ginger

2 tablespoons soy sauce
2 tablespoons Asian chili paste
    (available in supermarkets)
2 teaspoons Asian sesame oil

In a small bowl, whisk together all of the ingredients. Use immediately, or cover and store in the refrigerator for up to 2 days.

*Makes about 1 cup, or enough for up to 3 pounds of meat, poultry, seafood, or vegetables*

# Southwestern Marinade

An excellent marinade for London Broil (page 48); also good for chicken, pork, or shrimp.

6 cloves garlic, peeled and chopped
2 tablespoons finely grated lime zest
    (from 4 to 6 limes)
3/4 cup freshly squeezed lime juice
    (from 4 to 6 limes)
6 tablespoons canola oil, or other
    vegetable oil

1 tablespoon hot red pepper flakes
1 tablespoon ground cumin
1 1/2 teaspoon coarse salt, such as kosher
    salt

In a small bowl, whisk together all of the ingredients. Use immediately, or cover and store in the refrigerator for up to 2 days.

*Makes about 1 1/4 cups, or enough for up to 3 1/2 pounds of meat, poultry, or seafood*

# Red Wine Marinade

For London Broil (page 48) and Steak Lover's Salad (page 49) and also good with lamb and portobello mushrooms.

½ cup dry red table wine
⅓ cup freshly squeezed orange juice
 (from 1 orange)
¼ cup extra-virgin olive oil
6 cloves garlic, peeled and chopped
1 shallot, peeled and chopped
4 teaspoons chopped sage leaves, or
 2 teaspoons ground sage

1 tablespoon packed dark brown sugar
2 teaspoons coarse salt, such as kosher
 salt
2 teaspoons freshly ground pepper
1 bay leaf

In a small bowl, whisk together all of the ingredients, making sure the sugar is dissolved. Use immediately, or cover and store in the refrigerator for up to 2 days.

*Makes about 1⅓ cups, or enough for up to 4 pounds of meat*

# Orange-Rosemary Marinade

Good with chicken and pork.

---

3 tablespoons finely grated orange zest
   (from 3 oranges)
2/3 cup freshly squeezed orange juice
   (from 2 oranges)
6 tablespoons canola oil, or other
   vegetable oil
1/4 cup chopped rosemary leaves, or
   2 tablespoons dried rosemary

3 tablespoons balsamic vinegar
1 1/2 teaspoons coarse salt, such as
   kosher salt
3/4 teaspoon freshly ground pepper
3/4 teaspoon hot red pepper flakes

---

In a small bowl, whisk together all of the ingredients. Use immediately, or cover and store in the refrigerator for up to 2 days.

*Makes about 1 1/2 cups, or enough for up to 4 pounds of chicken or pork*

# Honey-Mustard Marinade

Good with chicken and pork.

---

½ cup honey
¼ cup Dijon mustard
¼ cup freshly squeezed lemon juice
   (from 1 to 2 lemons)

4 teaspoons soy sauce
3 cloves garlic, peeled and chopped

---

In a small bowl, whisk together all of the ingredients. Use immediately, or cover and store in the refrigerator for up to 2 days.

*Makes about 1 cup, or enough for up to 3 pounds of chicken or pork*

# White Wine–Tarragon Marinade

Excellent for Grilled Chicken Breasts (page 55) and seafood.

3/4 cup white wine or white Vermouth

6 tablespoons extra-virgin olive oil

6 tablespoons freshly squeezed lemon
juice (from 2 lemons)

6 cloves garlic, peeled and chopped

2 tablespoons chopped tarragon leaves,
or 1 tablespoon dried tarragon

1 1/2 teaspoons coarse salt, such as
kosher salt

1 teaspoon freshly ground pepper

In a small bowl, whisk together all of the ingredients. Use immediately, or cover and store in the refrigerator for up to 2 days.

*Makes about 1 1/2 cups, or enough for up to 4 pounds of chicken or seafood*

# Caribbean Marinade

Hey, mon. No problem wit' dis marinade! Excellent with Marinated Pork Tenderloin (page 72), and also with chicken and seafood.

1 cup pineapple juice
1 tablespoon finely grated lime zest
　　(from 2 to 3 limes)
6 tablespoons freshly squeezed lime
　　juice (from 3 limes)
6 cloves garlic, peeled and chopped
1/4 cup canola oil, or other vegetable oil
2 tablespoons peeled, chopped fresh
　　ginger

2 tablespoons Caribbean-style hot
　　sauce, made with habanero or
　　Scotch bonnet peppers
2 teaspoons dark molasses
2 teaspoons coarse salt, such as
　　kosher salt

1 • In a small pot, simmer the pineapple juice for 10 to 15 minutes, until it is reduced by half. (You should have 1/2 cup left.) Remove from the heat, and cool to room temperature.

2 • In a small bowl, whisk together the reduced pineapple juice with all of the remaining ingredients. Use immediately, or cover and store in the refrigerator for up to 2 days.

*Makes about 1 1/3 cups, or enough for up to 3 1/2 pounds of pork, chicken, or seafood*

# Tandoori Rub and Marinade

Good with Grilled Chicken Breasts (page 55) and lamb. Pat the spice rub on the meat before spooning the marinade over it. The marinade will be thick.

### FOR THE SPICE RUB

| | |
|---|---|
| 2 tablespoons coarse salt, such as kosher salt | 1 tablespoon curry powder |
| | 1½ teaspoons ground cumin |

Mix together all of the ingredients in an airtight container and store at room temperature. Rub on meat just before marinating. This rub will keep for several months.

*Makes about ¼ cup, or enough for up to 3 pounds of chicken or lamb*

### FOR THE MARINADE

| | |
|---|---|
| ½ medium onion, peeled and chopped | ¼ cup peeled, chopped fresh ginger |
| ½ cup plain yogurt | ¼ cup chopped cilantro leaves |
| ¼ cup freshly squeezed lime juice (from 2 limes) | 4 cloves garlic, peeled and chopped |
| | 2 tablespoons peanut oil |

In a small bowl, whisk together all of the ingredients. Use immediately, or cover and store in the refrigerator for up to 2 days.

*Makes about 1¾ cups, or enough for up to 4 pounds of chicken or lamb*

# BBQ Rub

Here's a great basic rub to use on your ribs (pages 66–69) or your Pulled Pork (page 70) recipe. Don't use it for anything that you're going to cook over direct heat, because the sugar will burn and you'll be left with a carbonized piece of meat.

6 tablespoons packed light brown sugar
2 tablespoons chili powder
1 tablespoon paprika
1 tablespoon garlic powder
2 teaspoons onion powder
2 teaspoons coarse salt, such as kosher
  salt

2 teaspoons ground cumin
1 teaspoon ground cinnamon
1 teaspoon freshly cracked pepper
¹/₄ to ¹/₂ teaspoon cayenne pepper

Mix together all of the ingredients in an airtight container and store at room temperature. The rub will keep for several months.

*Makes about 1 cup, enough for 3 recipes Pulled Pork or 8 pounds of Memphis-Style Ribs (page 68)*

# Beef Rub

For Essential Beef Brisket (page 50), or other cuts of beef.

---

*¹/₄ cup packed light brown sugar*
*2 tablespoons chili powder*
*2 tablespoons garlic powder*

*2 tablespoons onion powder*
*1 tablespoon instant beef bouillon powder*
*¹/₄ teaspoon cayenne pepper*

---

Mix together all of the ingredients in an airtight container and store at room temperature. The rub will keep for several months.

*Makes about ³/₄ cup, or enough for 6 pounds of beef*

# Jerk Seasoning

Good with chicken (see Jerk Chicken, page 60) and pork.

---

1/4 cup pineapple juice

4 scallions, white and green parts chopped

3 cloves garlic, peeled and chopped

2 tablespoons Caribbean-style hot sauce, made with habanero or Scotch bonnet peppers

1 tablespoon packed dark brown sugar

1 teaspoon coarse salt, such as kosher salt

1 teaspoon ground cinnamon

1 teaspoon ground allspice

1/2 teaspoon dried thyme

---

In a small bowl, whisk together all of the ingredients. Use immediately, or cover and store in the refrigerator for up to 2 days.

*Makes about 1 cup, or enough for up to 4 pounds of chicken or pork*

# Beer Mop

Ninety-nine bottles of beer on the wall, 99 bottles of beer . . . I know you've got beer in the house. So what's not to like about this recipe? Use with Essential Beef Brisket (page 50) and any other beef or pork you want to flavor while grilling.

1 (12-ounce) bottle beer
1/2 cup cider vinegar
1 tablespoon garlic powder

1 tablespoon onion powder
1 tablespoon sugar
1 teaspoon hot red pepper flakes

1 • In a small bowl, mix together all of the ingredients, making sure the sugar is dissolved.
2 • Apply to meat on the grill as indicated in the recipe, using a barbecue mop (page 9), a pastry brush, a long-handled spoon, or a spray bottle.
3 • Use immediately, or cover and store in the refrigerator for up to 1 week.

*Makes about 2 cups*

# Wine Mop

This is an amusing little marinade with a bouquet that brings to mind hints of vinegar, garlic, and beef. Use with Essential Beef Brisket (page 50) and any other beef or pork you want to flavor while grilling.

*1 cup dry red table wine*
*1/2 cup red wine vinegar*
*1/2 cup low-sodium beef broth*

*1 tablespoon garlic powder*
*2 teaspoons chili powder*

1 • In a small bowl, whisk together all of the ingredients.
2 • Apply to meat on the grill as indicated in the recipe, using a barbecue mop (page 9), a pastry brush, a long-handled spoon, or a spray bottle.
3 • Use immediately, or cover and store in the refrigerator for up to 1 week.

*Makes about 2 cups*

# Cilantro-Mint Pesto

Good for shrimp (see Shrimp with Cilantro-Mint Pesto, page 85), Grilled Chicken Breasts (page 55), and firm, white-flesh fish fillets. Can be used either as a marinade or as a condiment.

1⅓ cups packed cilantro leaves
¾ cup packed mint leaves
½ cup extra-virgin olive oil
¼ cup freshly grated Parmesan cheese
¼ cup freshly squeezed lime or lemon
    juice (from 2 limes or 1 to 2
    lemons)

4 cloves garlic, peeled
1 jalapeño pepper, stemmed and seeded
1 teaspoon coarse salt, such as kosher
    salt

Combine all of the ingredients in the work bowl of a food processor or in a blender, and process until pureed. Use immediately, or cover and store in the refrigerator for up to 2 days.

*Makes 2 cups, or enough for up to 4 pounds of seafood or chicken*

# Peanut Dipping Sauce

Kids love this dipping sauce. You can get 'em to eat almost any veggie with it, because it's like having a peanut butter sandwich for dinner. Adults like it for dipping meat for the same reason. It is a must for Satay (page 76).

¾ cup unsweetened, canned coconut
    milk
1½ teaspoons Thai red curry paste
    (available in supermarkets)
1½ teaspoons Thai chili oil, or Chinese
    chili oil (available in supermarkets)
2 tablespoons creamy peanut butter

1½ teaspoons sugar
1 teaspoon lime juice (from 1 lime)
½ teaspoon salt

1 • In a small saucepan, bring the coconut milk to a boil over medium heat. Add the curry paste and the chili oil and stir for about 1 minute. Add the peanut butter, sugar, lime juice, and salt, and mix well. Simmer for 5 minutes, stirring frequently. Taste and add more sugar, lime juice, or salt as needed.

2 • Remove from the heat and cool to room temperature. Use immediately, or cover and store in the refrigerator for up to 2 days. Bring to room temperature before serving.

*Makes 1 cup, or enough for 2 pounds poultry or meat*

# Basic Vinaigrette

2 cloves garlic, peeled and minced
1 teaspoon coarse salt, such as kosher
    salt
$1/4$ teaspoon freshly ground pepper

$1/4$ cup red wine vinegar
2 tablespoons balsamic vinegar
$3/4$ cup extra-virgin olive oil

Place the garlic, salt, and pepper in a small bowl. Add the vinegars and whisk. Keep whisking, and pour the oil in slowly, so that it is incorporated into the dressing. Use immediately, or cover and store in the refrigerator for up to 2 days.

**VARIATIONS:** Before you add the oil, stir in 1 tablespoon of Dijon mustard, and/or 1 tablespoon chopped fresh herbs. Try different vinegars—white wine, cider, rice, or flavored vinegars—or different oils (such as walnut or hazelnut oil). Substitute lemon juice for all or some of the vinegar, or add 2 teaspoons finely grated citrus zest to the dressing.

*Makes 1$1/4$ cups*

# Caesar Dressing

6 tablespoons freshly squeezed lemon
    juice (from 2 lemons)
1/3 cup extra-virgin olive oil
6 cloves garlic, peeled
1/2 medium onion, peeled and cut into
    chunks

2 tablespoons anchovy paste
1/2 teaspoon dry mustard
Several dashes Worcestershire sauce
6 tablespoons freshly grated Parmesan
    cheese

Combine all of the ingredients except the cheese in the work bowl of a food processor or in a blender and process until very smooth. Add the cheese and process briefly. Use immediately, or cover and store in the refrigerator for up to 2 days.

*Makes about 1 1/2 cups*

# Rosemary Butter

8 tablespoons (1 stick) unsalted butter,
    at room temperature
3 tablespoons chopped rosemary leaves
1 teaspoon finely grated orange zest
    (from 1/2 orange)

1 clove garlic, peeled and minced
Salt
Freshly ground pepper

1 • In a medium bowl, stir the butter until it is very soft. Sprinkle the rosemary, orange zest, garlic, salt, and pepper evenly over the butter. Stir again to distribute the seasonings throughout the butter.

2 • Turn the butter out onto a piece of waxed paper and form it into a log about 5 inches long and 1 inch thick. Roll the waxed paper around the log, then roll the log again in plastic wrap, twisting the ends to seal.

3 • Refrigerate until well chilled; the butter will keep for up to 2 days. Alternatively, you can freeze the butter for up to 2 months. Defrost in the refrigerator overnight.

4 • To serve, cut into 1/2-inch slices and place on top of meat, poultry, fish, or vegetables hot off the grill.

**VARIATIONS:** Substitute tarragon, chives, basil, cilantro, or a mixture of herbs for the rosemary. Substitute lemon or lime zest for the orange zest.

*Makes 10 servings*

# Not-So-Basic BBQ Sauce

Okay. You want to make your own barbecue sauce because your brother-in-law goes on and on about his "secret sauce." Puhllleeeeeze! As I've said before, just doctor up some sauce off the shelf (see page 64). But if you must have a barbecue sauce to call your own, here's the one. They'll be trying to analyze this one for weeks. Don't tell 'em where you got it from. A great line that always gets a laugh if someone asks you for your recipe is: "I could tell you, but then I'd have to kill you."

4 tablespoons (1/2 stick) unsalted butter
1 medium onion, peeled and finely
    chopped
6 cloves garlic, peeled and minced
2 1/4 cups ketchup
1 cup strong, brewed coffee (don't use a
    flavored roast)

1/2 cup Worcestershire sauce
1/4 cup cider vinegar
1/4 cup dark molasses
2 tablespoons chili powder
1 tablespoon Louisiana-style hot sauce
Salt
Freshly ground pepper

1 • Melt the butter in a medium saucepan set over medium heat. Add the onion and sauté, stirring, for 3 to 5 minutes, until softened but not browned. Add the garlic and cook for 2 to 3 minutes more.

2 • Add the remaining ingredients and cook over low heat, with the saucepan partially covered, for 30 minutes, stirring occasionally.

3 • Remove the saucepan from the heat, and cool the sauce to room temperature. Taste and add more hot sauce, salt, and pepper, if needed.

4 • Use immediately, or cover and store in the refrigerator for up to 4 days. You can freeze the sauce in an airtight container for up to 2 months.

*Makes about 5 cups.*

# Bourbon-Peach BBQ Sauce

Once again, I caught your attention with alcohol. This is a great, sweet sauce with a little surprise.

6 tablespoons (³/₄ stick) unsalted
 butter
1 medium onion, peeled and finely
 chopped
6 cloves garlic, peeled and minced
1¹/₂ cups ketchup

1 cup plus 2 tablespoons bourbon
1 cup peach or apricot preserves
2 tablespoons chili powder
1¹/₂ teaspoons Louisiana-style hot sauce
Salt
Freshly ground pepper

1 • Melt the butter in a medium saucepan set over medium heat. Add the onion and sauté, stirring, for 3 to 5 minutes, until softened but not browned. Add the garlic and cook, stirring, for 2 to 3 minutes more.

2 • Add the remaining ingredients and cook over low heat for 30 minutes, with the saucepan partially covered, stirring occasionally.

3 • Remove the saucepan from the heat and cool the sauce to room temperature. Taste and add more hot sauce, salt, or pepper, if needed.

4 • Use immediately, or cover and store in the refrigerator for up to 4 days. You can freeze the sauce in an airtight container for up to 2 months.

*Makes about 5 cups*

# Kitchen Sink BBQ Sauce

This is the way I like to cook. You go to the fridge and the pantry and see what you've got in there. Then you devise a recipe to fit the ingredients. This one will use most of what you've got in your spice rack with good results.

*¹/₄ cup canola oil, or other vegetable oil*
*1 medium onion, peeled and finely chopped*
*6 cloves garlic, peeled and minced*
*¹/₂ green bell pepper, stemmed, seeded, and finely chopped*
*¹/₂ red bell pepper, stemmed, seeded, and finely chopped*
*2 cups ketchup*
*1 (12-ounce) bottle store-bought chili sauce*
*1 cup cola*
*¹/₄ cup Worcestershire sauce*
*¹/₄ cup cider vinegar*
*3 tablespoons dark molasses*
*3 tablespoons chili powder*
*1 tablespoon paprika*
*1 tablespoon dry mustard*
*1 teaspoon ground cumin*
*¹/₂ teaspoon cayenne pepper*
*Salt*

1 • Heat the oil in a medium saucepan set over medium heat. Add the onion and sauté, stirring, for 3 to 5 minutes, until softened but not browned. Add the garlic and cook, stirring, for 2 to 3 minutes more. Add the green and red bell peppers and cook, stirring, for 5 minutes, until they begin to soften.

2 • Add all of the remaining ingredients, except for the salt, and stir well. Cook, with the saucepan partially covered, over medium-low heat for 20 to 30 minutes, stirring occasionally. Remove the saucepan from the heat and cool the sauce to room temperature. Taste, and add salt and more cayenne, if needed.

3 • Use immediately, or cover and store in the refrigerator for up to 4 days. You can freeze the sauce in an airtight container for up to 2 months.

*Makes 5 to 6 cups*

# Vinegar Sauce

Serve with Memphis-Style ("dry") Ribs (page 68), or as an alternative to regular BBQ sauce with Pulled Pork (page 70).

2 cups cider vinegar
1/4 cup ketchup
2 tablespoons packed dark brown sugar
1 tablespoon salt

1 tablespoon Louisiana-style hot sauce
2 teaspoons freshly ground pepper
1 teaspoon chili powder

In a medium bowl, whisk together all of the ingredients. Use immediately, or cover and store in the refrigerator for up to 1 week.

*Makes about 2 1/2 cups*

# Sources

## GRILLS AND ACCESSORIES

### WEBER GRILLS

WEBER-STEPHEN PRODUCTS CO.

200 EAST DANIELS ROAD

PALATINE, IL 60067

(800) 446-1071

WWW.WEBERBBQ.COM

### BARBEQUES GALORE

15041 BAKE PARKWAY, SUITE A

IRVINE, CA 92618

(800) 752-3085

WWW.BBQGALORE-ONLINE.COM

### WILLIAMS-SONOMA

3250 VAN NESS AVENUE

SAN FRANCISCO, CA 94109

(800) 541-2233

WWW.WILLIAMS-SONOMA.COM

### CHEF'S CATALOG

151A SKOKIE BOULEVARD

NORTHBROOK, IL 60035

(800) 338-3232

WWW.CHEFSCATALOG.COM

### GRILL LOVER'S CATALOG

BOX 1300

COLUMBUS, GA 31902

(800) 241-8981

WWW.GRILLLOVERS.COM

### PEOPLES WOODS

75 MILL STREET

CUMBERLAND, RI 02864

(800) 729-5800

WWW.PEOPLESWOODS.COM

## SPICES AND RUBS

### DEAN & DELUCA

ATTN: CUSTOMER SERVICE

2526 EAST 36TH STREET NORTH CIRCLE

WICHITA, KS 67219

(877) 826-9246

WWW.DEANDELUCA.COM

### PENZEYS SPICES

BOX 933

MUSKEGO, WI 53150

(800) 741-7787

WWW.PENZEYS.COM

### EL PASO CHILE COMPANY

909 TEXAS AVENUE

EL PASO, TX 79901

(888) 472-5727

WWW.ELPASOCHILE.COM

## REGIONAL SAUCES

### SCOTTS BARBECUE SAUCE

(800) 734-7282

WWW.SCOTTSBBQSAUCE.COM

EASTERN CAROLINA

### PETER'S BEACH BARBEQUE SAUCE

(800) 359-7873

WWW.PETERSBEACHSAUCES.COM

WESTERN CAROLINA

### MAURICE'S CAROLINA GOLD

(800) 628-7423

WWW.MAURICESBBQ.COM

SOUTH CAROLINA

### MOONLITE BAR-B-Q

(270) 684-8143

WWW.MOONLITE.COM

KENTUCKY

**WILLINGHAM'S**

(800) 737-9426

WWW.WILLINGHAMS.COM

MEMPHIS, TENNESSEE

**ARTHUR BRYANT'S**

(816) 231-1123

WWW.RBJB.COM

KANSAS CITY, MISSOURI

**SONNY BRYAN'S**

(214) 357-7120

WWW.SONNYBRYANSBBQ.COM

TEXAS

## ECLECTIC SAUCES AND CONDIMENTS

**JACK'S BBQ**

(760) 347-9435

WWW.JACKSBBQ.COM

CALIFORNIA

**RIVER RUN**

(802) 863-0499

WWW.RIVERRUNSOUL.COM

VERMONT

**STONEWALL KITCHEN**

(800) 207-5267

WWW.STONEWALLKITCHEN.COM

MAINE

**AMERICAN SPOON FOODS**

(800) 222-5886

WWW.SPOON.COM

MICHIGAN

## SPECIALTY MEATS

### ALLEN BROTHERS

3737 SOUTH HALSTED STREET

CHICAGO, IL 60609-1689

(800) 957-0111

WWW.ALLENBROTHERS.COM

### GEORGETOWN FARM

BOX 558, RR 1, BOX 14W

MADISON, VA 22727

(540) 948-4209

EMAIL: INFO@EATLEAN.COM

### SUMMERFIELD FARM

10044 JAMES MONROE HIGHWAY

CULPEPPER, VA 22701

(800) 898-3726

EMAIL: SFP@MNSINC.COM

### AIDELLS SAUSAGE COMPANY

1625 ALVARADO STREET

SAN LEANDRO, CA 94577

(800) 546-5795

WWW.AIDELLS.COM

### NIMAN RANCH

1025 EAST 12TH STREET

OAKLAND, CA 94606

(510) 808-0330

WWW.NIMANRANCH.COM

### JOHNSONVILLE SAUSAGE

BOX 906

SHEBOYGAN, WI 53085

(888) 556-BRAT

WWW.JOHNSONVILLE.COM

## SPECIALTY SEAFOOD

### BROWNE TRADING COMPANY

MERRILL'S WHARF

260 COMMERCIAL STREET

PORTLAND, ME 04101

(800) 944-7848

WWW.BROWNETRADING.COM

## EVENTS AND INFORMATION

----------------------------------------

### NATIONAL BARBECUE NEWS

WWW.BARBECUENEWS.COM

CALENDAR LISTING OF COOK-OFFS AND

FESTIVALS WORLDWIDE

### BARBECUE'N ON THE

### INTERNET

WWW.BARBECUEN.COM

FOR THE TRUE ENTHUSIAST

# Index

marinades (*cont.*)

    Caribbean, 172

    honey-mustard, 170

    orange-rosemary, 169

    red wine, 168

    and rub, tandoori, 173

    Southwestern, 167

    white wine–tarragon, 171

marinated pork tenderloin, 72

Maurice's Carolina Gold, 190

Mazzeo's Meat Market, 11

meat:

    resources for, 192

    *see also specific meats*

melon-mango-berry salad, 128–29

Memphis in May Barbecue Championship,

    xv-xvi

Memphis-style ribs, 68–69

mesquite chips, 7

mint-cilantro pesto, 179

    shrimp with, 85

mint lemonade, 161

mitts, 9

mix-ins, for ice cream, 149

mocha brownies, 133

monkfish, in fish fillets with lemon-parsley sauce,

    80–81

Monterey Jack cheese:

    in grilled quesadillas, 30

    in skillet corn bread, two ways, 120–21

    in your basic burgers, 35

Moonlite Bar-B-Q, 190

mop:

    beer, 177

    for sauce, 9–10

    wine, 178

mushrooms:

    domestic, grilled, 109

    portobello, grilled, 109

mushrooms (*cont.*)

    portobello, in vegetarian burgers, 40–41

mussels and clams, grill-steamed, 88–89

mustard-honey marinade, 170

my mom's peas and rice, 96

National Barbecue News, 193

National Hot Dog and Sausage Council, 42

Navy beans, in best baked beans, 94–95

nectarines, grilled, 127

Neely brothers, xvi

New Orleans–style barbecued shrimp, 86–87

New York strip steak, 45

Niman Ranch, 192

no-fuss frosted brownies, 133

not-so-basic BBQ sauce, 184

not your usual burgers, 39

nut(s):

    brownies, 133

    peanut butter-chocolate chip cookie ice

        cream sandwiches, 146–47

    peanuts, honey-roasted, in BBQ popcorn, 27

    toasting of, 97

    wild rice salad with toasted almonds, 97

    *see also* peanut dipping sauce

olive-chile dip, 23

onion(s):

    dip, homemade, 26

    red, and cucumber salad, 117

    red, grilled, 110

    Spanish, grilled, 110

    Vidalia, grilled, 110

orange-rosemary marinade, 169

Parmesan cheese:

    in Caesar dressing, 182

    in chicken Caesar salad with grilled croutons,

        56–57